This book is published by
Grosvenor House Publishing Ltd
28-30 High Street, Guildford, Surrey, GU1 3HY.
www.grosvenorhousepublishing.co.uk

A CIP record for this book
is available from the British Library

ISBN 978-1-906645-58-8

Falaise Castle & Matilda's Fountain

Peter Fieldman

1066 The Conquest

"Nothing that has gone before has been so daunting
Nothing that comes after will be so decisive"

Sources

The Anglo Saxon Chronicles
The Viking Ship Museum Oslo
The Tapestry Museum in Bayeux
Scenes from the XI century Bayeux Tapestry reproduced with
special authorisation and courtesy of the Town of Bayeux
XIX century prints from Histoire de France by Henri Martin

Acknowledgements

History is the path to the future.
I extend my gratitude for helping me to bring these events to life:
To my wife Lucia for having put up with me for so long working on this project
To our friend Anke for the use of her Mediterranean apartment where I found inspiration
To Paul Fieldman for his collaboration and computer design skills
To the cooperation of the City of Bayeux
To the Cafe Hugo in Paris where I spent so much time revising the manuscript

"All men dream: but not equally. Those who dream by night in the dusty recesses of their minds wake in the day to find that it is vanity. But the dreamers of the day are dangerous men for they act their dreams with open eyes to make it possible."
T. E. Lawrence

*O*ne thousand years ago
on one of the most important
dates in English history the
illegitimate son of a Norman
Duke became King of England.

*F*rom his appointment as Duke
of Normandy at the age of eight
on the death of his father he
survived attempts on his life and
grew up in a medieval world full of
intrigue, treachery and vengeance.

*A*fter years of conflict he
became the most powerful leader
of his time, entering into a marriage
opposed by the Pope that endured
thirty years.

*H*e gained the friendship of his greatest rival Harold, the Saxon Earl, until the final confrontation on the field near Hastings gave him the crown.

*T*he events leading to the last invasion of England have been preserved for eternity in a remarkable coloured embroidery dating from the 11th century known as the Bayeux Tapestry without which this story could not be told.

*T*his is the legend of William the Conqueror.

Preface

On the 6th January 1066 Harold Godwinson, Earl of Wessex, was crowned King of England. His reign was short lived. Ten months later he was lying dead in an English field. The man who succeeded him was a Norman called William or, to give him his correct title, Guillaume, Duke of Normandy. All these facts can be found in the Saxon Chronicles.

But the real story of the Norman invasion and how William came to claim the throne of England has been recorded for posterity in a unique seventy metre long, coloured embroidery known throughout the world as the Bayeux Tapestry. This extraordinary visual interpretation of the events leading up to the Battle of Hastings, dating from the eleventh century and incorporating action scenes with elements of medieval life, has survived for a thousand years despite wars, political upheaval and revolutions. Initially credited to William's wife, Matilda of Flanders, it is believed to be the work of Kentish craftsmen undertaken sometime between 1070 and 1077.

Although the rise to power of William in Normandy and Harold's influence in England spanned in excess of two decades, the story depicted in the Tapestry is limited to the two year period between 1064 and 1066. Despite the mystery and controversy surrounding the Tapestry's creator, it was most likely commissioned by Odo (or Odon) de Conteville, Bishop of Bayeux, and the Conqueror's half brother, after his appointment as Earl of Kent, to be exhibited in Bayeux Cathedral.

If the dates are correct, it was a remarkable achievement that a decade after the invasion Bishop Odo managed to convey, either from memory or from a diary that he had compiled, a precise description set out in the form of an extraordinary coloured comic strip, divided into fifty eight separate scenes, of the circumstances leading up to what was arguably one of the greatest military expeditions of its time.

This is an account of the events depicted in the Bayeux Tapestry and those that led up to the battle. It is the story of two men, one Saxon, the other Norman, both claiming the throne of England, whose destinies were to lead to a final confrontation on an English hillside that changed the course of English history. It also portrays the love between two people in a marriage that lasted for more than thirty years and was deemed to have remained a faithful union, which, during one of the most tempestuous periods of our time, produced ten children.

The battle of Hastings and the death of Harold Godwinson, the King of England mortally wounded, so legend has it, by a stray Norman arrow which pierced his eye, are part of English folklore. But what do we know about William, the man destined to be King? He was the illegitimate son of a Norman Duke, propelled into the role of Duke of the Duchy when he was only eight. From this point on, history tells us he grew up to be a faithful husband, a devoted father, an able administrator, a pious Christian and a ruthless warlord. Moreover, at thirty-nine years old, with not a drop of English blood in his veins, he became King and undisputed ruler of England as well as of his native Normandy.

While William's achievements and brutality as King of England between 1066 and 1087 are well documented, there has been relatively little interest shown in the origins of this charismatic figure from Normandy, who after two decades of intrigue, rivalry and conflict, defeated rebellious Barons and warmongering neighbours to establish a highly organised and efficient feudal system with the support of the church. Having managed to overcome the inner conflict arising from his illegitimate origin as well as political rivalry and military resistance from his opponents, he brought peace to his Duchy and then persuaded soldiers, peasants, mercenaries and adventurers from across Europe to join his armada and undertake a risky and perilous expedition to invade England and claim the crown. For this reason, the year 1066 remains engraved on the mind of every schoolchild as the most important date in English history.

Introduction

By the beginning of the eleventh century, the Normans, men from the north, who were descendants of the Vikings, had established one of the most powerful and warlike states in Christendom. Their influence extended to Spain and as far as Sicily. It was a period that saw great changes taking place across the world. Even as armed conflicts led to the rise and fall of regimes and monarchies, art and religion were becoming established aspects of society. In Spain El Cid would push back the Moors leading ultimately to its reunification; the Byzantine Empire extended from Constantinople throughout the Middle East; it was the Heian period in Japan, ruled from Kyoto, the capital city where Buddhism was reaching the masses; a new class of warrior, whose legacy remains to this day, became established - the Samourai. Neighbouring China was controlled by the Song Dynasty, the Maya civilisation was predominant in Central America and in Rome the Pope was extending his power and influence on society as the Christian church began to spread into the Feudal societies, expanding across Europe and even taking an active role in military conflicts.

As descendants of the Vikings the Normans had inherited a fighting spirit and brought with them a new style of offensive warfare unknown in Saxon and Viking occupied England. Their strategy relied on the mobility of mounted knights armed with lances and swords, able to sweep into battle at speed and adapt to changing tactics of enemy forces quickly. The cavalry was supported by bowmen, lined up in close formation, concentrating their fire power by unleashing a barrage of arrows into the sky to rain down on opponents like modern mortar or artillery fire. It was also the beginning of the age of stone built castles; impregnable strongholds built to secure the possession and occupation of conquered territory that would play an essential role in the expansion of Norman influence.

England, at this time, found itself torn by rivalry between Saxons, Vikings and Celts each controlling different regions of the country and claiming the throne for one of their own. Such was the danger to King Aethelred, that the Queen, Emma, sent her two children, Alfred and Edward, to seek refuge with her brother, Duke Robert I, in Normandy. Following Aethelred's death in 1016, while her children were growing up in Normandy, Emma re- married, this time to Cnut, the new King from Denmark and she bore him a son, Hardicanute.

It was into this changing world that in the year of our Lord 1027 in the castle at Falaise, a village in Normandy, a child named William was born. His father, Robert the Magnificent, son of Robert 1, had become Duke of Normandy, after the mysterious death of his brother. His mother, Herleva, known as Arlette, was the daughter of Fulbert, a tanner to the Court. Although Christians, living as man and wife, they had not taken the vows of marriage, and as William grew up he had to face opposition from the church and confront the many power-ful Norman Barons who would not serve a future Duke born out of wedlock. No one could have foreseen that nearly forty years later these unrelated events would lead to the conquest of England by the ruler of the Duchy of Normandy.

PART I

CHAPTER 1

The fighting had ceased and there was an eerie silence hanging over the hillside. Dusk and the stench of rotting corpses were making the recovery of bodies laborious, made even more distasteful by the looting of clothing, mail, helmets, personal items and weapons. A tall well built man, not yet forty, his face and chain mail splattered with blood, was walking around the battlefield, lingering from time to time to observe one of the many bodies strewn across the hillside. For William, Duke of Normandy, the 14th October 1066 had been a long and bloody day. When he finally reached the ridge, some of his foot soldiers were already grouped around the Saxon position where the Norman standard had been planted firmly into the ground. They were staring down at the body of a Saxon warrior. He was lying on his back, his arms by his side, his legs straight. The chain mail had turned red with gaping holes where Norman broadswords had pierced it. The soldiers parted when they saw the Duke approaching to let him through. He stood for a moment over the body then knelt down. The man's helmet concealed most of his face. William took the helmet in his hands and gently removed it allowing the man's long hair to drape over his shoulders. His face was distorted and bloody with a hole where his right eye had been. William placed his hand on the man's forehead and looked up at the sky. He knew his calculated gamble had paid off. Nobody could stand in his way to take the crown of England; the bastard, who had become a Duke while still a child, would now be a King.

CHAPTER 2

It was the 9th September 1089. Two years to the day had passed since King William 1 had died at Rouen. Even after twenty one years on the throne of England he had never forgotten that he was still Duke of Normandy and in 1087 had to return to quell yet another revolt, this time at Mantes, a town on the bank of the river Seine, some 50 kilometres from Paris. It was to be his last battle. Flames rising from buildings set ablaze by William's troops caused his horse to panic. As it reared up, William was propelled forward and thrown to the ground by the sudden movement. Norman saddles were designed with high pommels to give stability to riders in battle. They were not meant to stop a human body, especially one that was heavy and since the death of his wife Matilda in 1083, William had become grossly over-weight. He hit the pommel with such force it ruptured his blood vessels causing internal bleeding. He was taken to his palace at Rouen and then to the Priory of St Gervais, where after a month in agony, in the presence of two of his sons, William and Henry, he died. It was an ignominious ending for the King of England. After several weeks of uncertainty his body was finally taken by sea to Caen and laid to rest in the Abbey of St Etienne. The reign of the most powerful War Lord in Christendom was over.

On that autumn day of 1089 in Normandy it was windy and raining heavily. It had been a long and tiring journey for the three horsemen, dressed in black cloaks, their heads covered by hoods to provide some protection from the elements, as they made their way slowly along the track that led to Bayeux. Reaching the village, their appearance and the sound of horses' hooves splashing through the muddy, narrow alleys, did not go unnoticed by the local peasants going about their daily chores.

The horsemen halted when they reached the west façade of the cathedral. The Norman built sanctuary, standing majestically before them, had been constructed in the Romanesque style from stone quarried near Caen in 1062. The forbidding symmetrical towers with their solid, stone walls rose vertically for more than twenty-five metres. To support the vaulted roof and high walls, buttresses had been built at intervals along each side. One of the men seemed to take a special interest in this house of God, looking up at the large arched opening above the central porch between the towers. The silence was broken by one of his companions.

"Well, Sire, we are here at last."

Without replying the man dismounted and handed the reins of his horse to his companion. Shaking the rain off his cloak, he slowly made his way up the path towards the entrance of the cathedral. He pushed one of the great doors, but it did not budge.

Inside, a monk kneeling in prayer heard the noise outside, shuffled to the entrance and pulled open one of the heavy oak doors. He looked down at the sandals of the man facing him and remarked on his soaked feet. His eyes rose, taking in the long black cloak tied with a cord. He saw before him a bearded man of about sixty, roughly one metre seventy. A little overweight, the monk thought to himself. The eyes though were still sharp. As the man removed his hood the monk stepped back in shock.

"Bishop Odo!"

"Let me pass," said the stranger impatiently.

The monk stood transfixed as the man brushed past him and walked down the left aisle of the cathedral. He was looking around, glancing into each of the shadowy chapels lining the aisles and up at the vaulted ceiling as he strode towards the bishop's throne by the high altar, almost slipping on the stone floor. In his wet clothing, Odo could feel the cold, damp air inside the cathedral permeating through his garments. He gave the impression of someone who knew exactly where he was going. Other monks, carrying out their duties, gazed at him as he passed and expressed the same look of surprise as their brother.

"Odo is back," whispered one Monk to his companions.

The news quickly spread around the sanctuary. After kneeling for a moment before the altar in silent prayer, Odo rose to his feet, glanced down the central nave, and walked back to the aisle until he reached an arched opening in the wall. He entered and disappeared from view. The sound of his wet sandals echoed as he descended the stone steps into the cathedral crypt.

Inside the crypt, the flickering flames from torches projected distorted shadows on the walls. A novice was sweeping the floor, quietly reciting prayers. At the sound of footsteps he stopped and looked up. The shadow of the visitor spread out in front of him.

"There is nobody here," he announced to the stranger, now facing him and looking around as if expecting to see someone.

"I am here, I am Odo of Conteville, Bishop of this cathedral."

The novice dropped his broom in surprise.

"I am sorry my Lord, I know you not. But I have heard of you."

"I have been away too long, first in England and then five years in a dungeon at Rouen because of my brother. But now he is dead, God rest his soul, I have my freedom."

Odo turned and gazed quizzically at the novice. He could not have been older than eighteen, his boyish face suggesting someone even younger and the monk's habit could not hide his skinny frame.

"You have been here long?"

"Just six months, my Lord."

Odo strode towards the far wall of the crypt. "Come, come with me."

Without hesitating the novice followed him. The crypt was no larger than ten square meters divided into three naves. The ribbed, vaulted arches were supported by eight circular pillars crowned with sculptured capitals decorated with frescoes of angels. Embedded in the centre of the far wall was an opening covered by a steel door about seventy centimetres square. Odo took two keys from his robe and handed them to the novice.

"Here, open the vault for me."

The novice looked startled but held out his hand and took the keys. In the obscurity of the crypt he had not paid any attention to the small door concealed in the wall. Now, lit by the torch, the vault stood out, he thought, like a tomb. After fiddling with the key he managed to insert it into the rusting lock and twisted it. He pulled, but it would not budge. As he pulled again, using more force, the heavy steel door slowly began to open with a scraping sound caused by its rusty hinges. The dust rising in the confined space made the novice sneeze. He covered his nose with his hand as he eased the door back against the wall as far as it would go before peering inside. As his eyes gradually became accustomed to the darkness he made out what appeared to be a large box.

"There is a something inside. It looks like a trunk of some sorts."

"I know," replied Odo impatiently. "Take it out."

Together they heaved out a heavy, dusty, wooden chest and eased it down to the floor. Odo's eyes began to gleam as he brushed off the mould and cobwebs that had found a home in the damp, black recess.

"Open it with the other key."

The novice did as he was asked, inserting the key and raising the catch. Cautiously lifting the top of the chest he peered inside and saw what looked like a rolled up parchment.

"Now, lift it out, but carefully," said Odo, his voice expressing excitement. "It is fragile."

As they unrolled the first section of the parchment it became clear that they were looking at an embroidered linen cloth woven in strips with exquisitely stitched woollen designs and figures with inscriptions sewn together and dyed a variety of colours. Although only about fifty centimetres in width, it appeared to be long, very long.

"Thank God it has been preserved," exclaimed Odo with relief.

"What is this meant to represent?" asked the novice as he examined with growing awe the coloured panels that seemed to illustrate a variety of scenes. Odo was running his hands delicately over the cloth to satisfy himself that it was not damaged.

"It is a glimpse of history. It chronicles the events leading to the invasion of England by my half brother, William, Duke of Normandy, in 1066. Before you were born."

"You were with Duke William in England?" The novice spoke with admiration.

"Oh yes, as his kinsman I was with him from the beginning."

"I would like to know more," said the novice eagerly.

Odo began to unroll the first section of the tapestry uncertain as to whether he should be flattered or bothered by the novice's increasing curiosity. Better to be grateful, he thought.

"See," he said, pointing to the Latin text, reading it aloud.

"Edward Rex Ubi Harold Dux Anglorum"

With the novice paying close attention, Odo started to explain the significance of the illustrated tapestry.

"It begins with King Edward of England who had no heir, asking the Saxon, Earl Harold, to visit Normandy to advise William that he had chosen him to succeed him."

The novice turned to Odo and shrugged his shoulders.

"So what led to the invasion?"

Odo placed his hand on the novice's shoulder.

"Come, sit down. It is a long story."

They made themselves as comfortable as possible on the stone floor close to the wooden chest. Odo's joy at finding the tapestry intact in the damp crypt made him forget how uncomfortable he was in the wet clothes clinging to his body. He crossed his legs and sat in silence for a while wondering how to answer the novice's question.

He and his brother, Robert of Mortain, were half brothers to William. Having been appointed Bishop of Bayeux by William in 1049 when just fifteen, Odo had been a faithful companion to his brother throughout the rebellious years in Normandy. He had dedicated himself to the church and had grown up to become one of the most eminent religious leaders in Normandy whose influence over the development of the church extended to both Normandy and England.

After William had conquered England, Odo's loyalty had been rewarded with large estates in Southeast England and the title of Earl of Kent. At the same time, he retained both his title and position as Bishop of Bayeux and had returned to Normandy on many occasions. But once the Kentish craftsmen had begun work on his embroidered account of the Norman invasion, completing it became an obsession, taking up far more of his time than he could afford.

Odo was constantly controlling the quality of the work and as it progressed had to ensure that the designs were an accurate reflection of the facts. It had been a massive task and Odo must have wondered how he was going to ship the final version back to Normandy. Nevertheless, the wooden chest in which it had been stored was taken from Canterbury to the coast with an escort of soldiers and loaded on board a longship, where it was carefully protected and strapped to the deck for the voyage. On arrival in Normandy, still under the watchful eye of Odo, it was transported to Bayeux Cathedral. Although he had decreed in 1077 that the completed tapestry was to be displayed in the cathedral once a year, circumstances and long periods of absence had prevented him from fulfilling his wish. However, Odo's relationship with William, the King, had gradually deteriorated in England and he was still not ready to forgive his brother for condemning him to five long years in Rouen prison.

"Perhaps I did make mistakes and should not have extracted so much money from the Saxons," he thought to himself. "But to deserve such a punishment from my own kinsman after all I had done!"

But now he had at last come back. Keeping his memories and his bitterness to himself, Odo's thoughts returned to the tapestry and the young novice. He was justly proud of his work and had found someone to whom he could relate his story.

Twenty-three years had gone by. He was a man of God. He knew that he and all those who had played a part in the invasion and had fought at the battle of Hastings would eventually pass on to another world, to be forgotten. Only the contents of the chest would be left for future generations to discover how the Normans had invaded and conquered England. As the novice listened attentively, Odo's voice began to echo around the crypt.

"Edward had spent his youth in Normandy before he became King of England. He and Duke William were kinsmen of sorts through the marriage of Edward's mother, Queen Emma to King Aethelred. She was the sister of William's grandfather Duke Robert, and thus William's great aunt. But if William believed he was the rightful successor, so did the Viking King, Hardrada and the powerful Saxons, Earl Godwin and his son Harold, who also claimed the throne for themselves. Conflict was inevitable."

Odo pondered for an instant and then continued.

"But William's destiny had been sealed many years before. When his father, Duke Robert, died on a pilgrimage to Jerusalem, William was only eight years old. The Duke had never married his mother, Arlette, who was not of noble origin, and there were many powerful Norman Barons who refused to be ruled by a child born out of wedlock."

Odo paused again and looked towards the young novice who was listening attentively.

"Several attempts were made on his life."

CHAPTER 3

It was a warm, sunny, summer afternoon in the year 1035 on the coast of Normandy. There was a slight breeze, which played with the tufts of reeds sprouting out of the dunes. The shore was flat, extending for several kilometres to both the east and west. Behind the dunes the ground sloped up gently at first before rising sharply to the line of trees at the edge of the forest.

Playing alone on the shore was a small, thin boy about eight years old, throwing pebbles into the sea and making patterns in the sand. The breeze blew his blond hair across his face masking his clear blue eyes. He looked puzzled when the waves lapping onto the shore broke over his feet and then receded, washing away his designs, leaving only a mound of wet sand split by streaks of water.

One hundred metres away at the foot of a rock strewn path, which climbed at an angle towards the trees and provided the only access to the sea shore, a young woman was seated on a horse-drawn wagon busy with her embroidery. Edwige was a simple girl with short, brown, untidy hair atop a plain face and at twenty, still single. She was, though, more than content to have been asked to look after young William. It was easier work than toiling in the fields and gave her time to engage in her favourite pastime, embroidery. A local girl, brought up in the pleasant, rolling countryside of Normandy, she was dressed in a long, black frock and white pinafore with a matching scarf tied around her head, typically worn by domestic servants. From time to time she looked up to glance at the child playing by the water's edge.

Neither of them was aware of two scruffy looking men watching their movements from the top of a dune. Lying flat on the sand, their bodies concealed behind a clump of bushes, they were unshaven and their poorly fitting clothes were torn. Their eyes had been following the playful antics of the boy on the sand.

"Long way from home ain't he," said the first man.

His companion sniggered. "He should know better than be out alone. Let's finish the job and claim our reward."

Gathering their swords both men started to slide cautiously down the dune towards the shore.

The young boy, busy watching the waves swirling around his feet, did not sense their presence until he suddenly saw two shadows appear in the water before him. Surprised, he turned around to find himself face to face with the armed strangers.

"Oh!" he exclaimed, visibly scared, his thin legs trembling.

At the same time the maid, who had been watching from a distance, also saw the two men approaching the boy. She dropped her work and cried out.

"William! What is it William?"

The two men, now close to the boy, instinctively turned towards where the voice came from while one reached out to grab him. Strong hands took hold of the boy's arms. The boy, petrified, shut his eyes. There was a thud followed by a cry. As quickly as they had held him he felt the hands loosen their grip. The boy opened his eyes as the man, arms outstretched, his face contorted in a grimace, with blood seeping from his mouth, fell towards him. As he stepped aside, the body hit the ground, sending up a fountain of water. Two arrows were embedded in the man's back. His companion was already clambering as fast as he could up the side of a dune, every move hampered by his sandals sinking into the soft sand. As he reached the ridge a horseman suddenly appeared and, with a slash of his sword, cut him down. Already dead, the man's lifeless body rolled back down the dune coming to a halt in a hideous twisted form.

It had all happened in a few minutes. Shocked, the boy raised his eyes. He found himself looking straight at the forelegs of a horse. Its nostrils were so close he could feel its hot breath. He looked up at the horse's rider but saw only cold eyes peering through the slit in his helmet. Behind him three archers on horseback guarding their distance, were lowering their bows and carefully sliding unspent arrows back into their quivers. As the other horseman guided his mount down the dune, the maid was running towards William screaming. The first knight dismounted and ignoring the boy walked slowly past him turning over the body of the man. He glanced at his companion.

"Recognize them?"

"No. But their ragged attire suggests they are paid assassins," replied the second knight. Sheathing his sword, the first knight slowly removed his gauntlets and took off his helmet. "Well they have paid now."

The boy's expression changed from one of fear to relief.

The man standing before him was tall and muscular, in his mid thirties. His long, dark hair was blowing across his face, the long scar on his cheek was masked by a beard. The eyes that were staring at William were ice blue. Roger, Count de Beaumont, was William's kinsman and a loyal friend to his father. He turned to the boy and put his hand on his shoulder as the maid arrived panting. She took hold of the boy and brushed him down.

"William, are you alright?"

"Does his mother know that you journeyed here without an escort?" Count Roger enquired of her. Looking downcast the maid answered.

"She... she does, my Lord."

Count Roger put his arm around William and together they walked slowly along the beach. He remained silent for a few minutes before looking down at the young boy.

"God favoured you this time." He turned and looked disapprovingly at the maid. "It was good fortune that led us here."

The second knight interrupted.

"My Lord I think it time to depart if we are to reach Bayeux before nightfall."

Count Roger glanced up at the darkening sky, nodded his approval and turned to the maid. "How did you get here?"

The maid turned and pointed to the horse and wagon some hundred meters away.

"You came in that! Well, let's not waste more time."

The wagon carrying William and Edwige, who had a very worried look on her face, was being escorted by Count Roger and his bodyguards and finally reached Bayeux Palace an hour later. Daylight was fading as they made their way slowly through the gate into the courtyard, the wheels of the wagon grinding across the wooden planks of the bridge that lay over the stream below the walls. As soon as they had passed beneath the porch, the gates slammed shut behind them.

William's mother, Herleva, was seated head bowed in her chamber, her hands across her lap, when Roger, William and Edwige made their entrance. William ran towards her and hugged her tight. She was dressed in black and her eyes were filled with tears. The news of Duke Robert's death at Nicaea in Asia Minor while returning from his pilgrimage to Jerusalem had only reached them early that morning. Having consented to William spending the day by the sea she had asked Count Roger to find him and break the news. She could see from their faces that something was wrong.

The maid, her head bowed, looked worried.

"I am sorry my Lady, but..."

William's mother raised her hand.

"Don't concern yourself, there is nothing to worry about."

She clasped William in her arms and hugged him again.

"You have had a long day. I think it is time for you to sleep. Go with Edwige."

She gestured to the maid. "Take him."

Herleva kissed William goodnight as Edwige took his hand and led him out, closing the door behind her.

Alone with Roger, Herleva who preferred to be called by her nickname, Arlette, looked at him anxiously.

"What happened?"

Roger, keeping his voice low, expressed his concern.

"We arrived in time to prevent at best a kidnap, at worst a murder."

Arlette gasped. "A murder!"

"There were two of them, probably paid assassins. We took no chances and killed them. Robert had to fend off many enemies. Do you think they would think twice about challenging an eight year old? Whoever was behind this act knew that Robert would never return."

Arlette was shaking, her eyes still tearful. "But so soon"

Roger looked at her. "Traitors amongst our own kinsmen; those who never accepted that you and Robert did not take the vows of marriage. From now on we must be on our guard."

He put his hands on Arlette's shoulders.

"I know you are in mourning but William must be sworn in as Duke. The barons and clergy must be summoned and the Bishop informed that there will be a ceremony to conduct. Do I have your consent?"

Arlette nodded. "Did you tell William about his father?"

"No, No, I could not. Not after what happened. It is late, rest. Let me explain everything to William tomorrow at Falaise."

Roger kissed her on both cheeks and made his exit.

Arlette slowly crossed the room and stood by the window. She could hear the gurgling sound of water flowing in the stream outside. Her thoughts turned to the day nine years before when she had been washing clothes by the fountain on the bank of the stream below the walls of Falaise castle. She had felt her heart pounding when Duke Robert the Magnificent first approached her and their eyes met. Although she was only seventeen and a poor tanner's daughter, the Duke had fallen in love with her. Three times he had come to gaze at her until finally he approached and they conversed for the first time.

With her father's consent, she had willingly agreed to become his companion and lover, and her life had completely changed from the day she moved into the castle. But when she gave birth to a son, they still had not married according to the Christian faith, and William was consequently regarded a bastard. Still only in her mid twenties, Arlette's pretty face, blond hair and trim figure turned many a suitor's eye. But before he had departed Robert had arranged, as the local custom permitted, for her to be married to a loyal Norman baron, Count Herluin de Conteville, who would give her the respectability she deserved. Now Robert was dead she was deeply worried about the responsibility that had suddenly fallen on her eight year old son.

CHAPTER 4

The Normans were at the forefront of a revolution in the architecture of defensive strongholds, building stone fortresses on high ground with vast rectangular or circular keeps. Falaise castle, where William was born and spent his first years, was no exception, rising ominously on a rocky hilltop overlooking a valley. Directly below, a stream cut a path through the lush green fields before disappearing into the dense woodland. The castle's towering square keep could be seen from afar. Thick grey stone walls rising high into the sky above a sheer cliff made it an impenetrable fortress and would deter the most reckless of invaders.

Being an adventurous child, William knew every corner, stairwell, secret passage and chamber, except one; he had never been allowed into his father's private study. He was therefore surprised when Roger beckoned him to follow as he climbed the stone steps spiralling high into the tower. His surprise turned to hesitation when Roger took out a key and unlocked the door to his father's chamber.

"Don't be afraid, go in," he said, inviting William to enter.

William stepped inside the chamber with caution. His father was not there. Through the slit window a shaft of sunlight beamed across the floor fixing its point on shelves full of manuscripts. William's eyes followed the beam and then took in all the contents of the chamber. On the table in the centre of the room lay a sword, a helmet and numerous objects. On one wall hung a large almond shaped shield emblazoned with the heraldic arms of the House of Normandy – two gold lions on a red background. William walked slowly around the room gazing at his father's effects.

On a side table he noticed a chess set laid out ready for play. He picked up a piece and in silence turned it over in his hand. It resembled a king.

"I will teach you how to play one day," said Roger, trying hard to smile.

He knew the time had come to break the news of his father's death. His face now serious, he reached up and took a book from the shelf, flicking over the pages. What was he going to say to the young boy standing before him? He looked down at William. This child was going to be a Duke. Manhood would come faster than for others of his age. He would soon learn about, and have to come to terms with, the indignity of his illegitimate birth and the scorn of many peers. Moreover, if he was to succeed, he would have to endure pain and suffering.

"These belong to your father," he said softly, waving the book around the room. He paused for a moment before placing his hands on William's shoulders and looking him in the eyes.

"I have sad tidings to bring you. I must tell you that your father will never return from his long pilgrimage to Jerusalem. An illness struck him down during his journey and God has taken his soul to him. He was a dear friend as well as a kinsman. I mourn him and share your suffering. But it was God's will and we are bound to abide by it."

William, the shock and sadness apparent in his expression, listened in silence, his head bowed as he stared at the stone floor. Tears slowly filled his eyes. His mind went back to the last time he had seen his father. It had been in his bedchamber. He remembered how his father, wearing a pilgrim's robe, had held him in his arms and told him that he was leaving on a long journey to a far off place, the name of which he had not understood. He could see his father now, turning to wave as he and his mother watched from the ramparts until both horse and rider had disappeared from view into the valley.

William felt the Count's hand sympathetically patting him on his shoulder. Then the faltering voice he was listening to shifted to one of authority.

"Your father was a man of God but also a War Lord. He had to be. Now you must learn to be a War Lord. You have seen that there are some who do not wish you to succeed him; men who seek the Duchy for themselves. But Kinsmen like me, loyal to your father and mother, and to Normandy, will protect you."

William listened in silence. At one point his hand reached out to the table to touch the handle of the sword and he ran his thumb carefully along the blade.

"One day I will teach you how to use that too."

Interrupted by the sound of horses and voices outside, Roger edged towards the window and peered out into the courtyard to see what the commotion was.

Knights had begun to arrive at the castle. News of the consecration of William as the new Duke of Normandy had reached every corner of the Duchy. The Norman Standard was blowing in the wind high above the keep of the castle as Knights and barons mingled with peasants, creating a jam as they clattered across the narrow drawbridge. Trumpets sounded as they entered the courtyard where they dismounted and handed their horses to servants. As they were led to the stables, the guests made their way into the great hall. There was a buzz of excitement, tinged with remorse, as the groups of nobles, members of the clergy and other guests mingled, exchanged views and discussed the future of Normandy.

Roger turned from the window to William and took a leather pouch from his pocket. He opened it and extracted a medallion. It was about five centimetres in diameter, made of silver and in the centre was engraved a crucifix.

"This belonged to your father. He entrusted it to me before he left. Now it is yours. Wear it and God will protect you."

William carefully took the medallion. He held it for a moment in both hands feeling the small cross in the centre. He then placed it over his head and let it drop around his neck tucking it into his tunic.

Roger gently put his hand on his shoulder.

"The Barons gave an oath to your father. They are now assembling below to give their oath to you. Some may not accept you because your father and mother did not live according to the church but God has chosen you to bring unity to Normandy. You have not yet reached manhood but must take your father's place and learn to become a leader. Do not be afraid. I shall stand by your side. Remember always hold your head upright."

Roger handed him a large robe. "You must wear this. Try it on."

William took the deep red, velvet cloth with gold edges and draped it over his shoulders. It was far too large for him. Roger helped him adjust it, tightening the cord around the waist.

"There, you look perfect," he said encouragingly to William. "Now, the Barons are waiting." He stepped back smiling, waved his hand across his body and bowed. "After you, my Lord."

CHAPTER 5

Ever since he had become Duke in 1027 after the mysterious death of his brother, Duke Robert had nurtured an ambition to set off on a pilgrimage to Jerusalem. Over Christmas in 1034 he chose to hold court at his castle at Le Vaudreuil, one of his many residences, near Rouen, close to the river Seine. He had summoned the most influential Barons, many his own kinsmen, from across the Duchy, as well as leading clergymen. William Talvas, Ranulf de Briquessard, Neel de Saint Sauveur, Hamon de Creully, Grimoult de Plessis, Guy de Bourgogne, Raoul Taisson and others had journeyed to Le Vaudreuil; esteemed names that the young boy who was present, would learn to remember as he grew up.

Duke Robert's son William, who was just seven years old, was guest of honour. It was a moment of immense satisfaction to his mother, Arlette, who was proud to see her young son taking his place next to his father.

"I have called you here as it will be my last Christmas before I leave for the Holy Land," announced the Duke to an astonished assembly. Reactions were mixed: the Barons expressing concern that the Duke's long absence could be harmful to the cohesion of the Duchy, while the ecclesiastical guests were fully in support of his commitment to God. "My absence forces me to assure my succession," continued the Duke, turning to the child by his side. "I introduce my son William. He will be my successor. I want you to swear allegiance to him."

Robert was never to return from his pilgrimage.

CHAPTER 6

The Saxon Chronicles:
"Blithe-minded aye was the harmless king though he long ere,
of land bereft abode in exile wide on the earth when Knut over-
came the kin of Aethelred and the Danes wielded the dear king-
dom of Engle-land. Eight and twenty winters' rounds they
wealth dispensed."

Trumpets announced William's presence, as two men at arms, standing by the entrance, pulled open the heavy oak doors to the great reception hall. The vast room fell silent. The eyes of everyone present were fixed on the young boy, wearing the long robe, which dragged behind him as he walked slowly towards the throne. Some appeared consolatory, others indifferent. William looked nervously at the assembled barons all elegantly dressed in their finest robes and then up at the ceiling. The hall seemed so vast and high. From the balustrades of the first floor gallery overlooking the magnificent banqueting hall, hung an array of colourful banners representing the Norman coats of arms.

With Roger at his side, he slowly climbed the three steps to the platform and took his place on the throne next to his mother as she beckoned him to be seated. Roger remained standing. He gestured to the barons to gather below the throne. Two men stepped forward leaving the other barons to jostle for space behind them. One, a slim tallish figure, approaching thirty, with a rather melancholic face partly hidden by a beard, was Prince Edward of England. The other was a man of the church of about the same age, albeit smaller in stature. Robert Champart of Jumieges was of slight build, almost gaunt, with a pale face, his hair already thinning on top. The two men had known each other ever since Edward had been sent to Normandy as a ten year old child some twenty years before.

At the beginning of the eleventh century, the conflict in England between Saxons and Vikings had posed a serious threat to King Aethelred. His Queen, Emma, sister of the 5th Duke of Normandy, William's grandfather, had arranged for her sons, Prince Edward and Alfred, to seek refuge in Normandy at the Abbey of Jumieges. The imposing Benedictine Abbey on the banks of the Seine, founded in 654 AD, by Saint Philibert, had become one of the largest and most renowned religious centres in Europe. When he reached manhood, Alfred had returned to London where, within a short time, he died. Rumour had it that Earl Godwin, an influential Saxon, had deliberately lured him into a trap to have him assassinated. Edward, though, had remained in Normandy and having spent most of his childhood in the company of young men of the church, had immersed himself in the language and customs of the Duchy. England was a country he hardly knew but he was still a Saxon and now he was expected to pledge loyalty to his young Norman kinsman in a foreign land.

Roger had asked the Bishop of Fecamp, at fifty-three, one of Normandy's most eminent priests, to preside over the ceremony and he had travelled to Falaise accompanied by a young monk of about thirty years of age called Lanfranc. After bowing his head towards William the Bishop turned to face the assembled barons and raised his hands.

"The King of France."

Before the Bishop could speak, a servant's sudden announcement turned everybody's heads towards the doors of the great hall. King Henry I strode into the hall with his entourage. Although not tall, the man carried his crown well, possessing an undeniable physical presence. His short, cropped hair revealed a handsome face. He had succeeded to the throne of France on the death of his father King Robert "the Pious" in 1031 when he was twenty-three years old. During sixteen years of rule he had strengthened France's position by astute military alliances with his neighbours, Normandy and Maine, and through marriage. Flanders was a close ally because of the marriage of his sister Adele to Count Baldwin V, who would later become William's father in law. His first wife Matilda, daughter of German Emperor Konrad II, had died in 1034 and after the death of his second wife, Matilda of Frise, in 1043, he had married Anna, daughter of the Prince of Kiev. She bore him a son, Philippe, who would succeed him as King. Henry had been a loyal friend to William's father, Duke Robert. As his overlord he now extended this friendship to the child who was about to take his father's place as the Duke of Normandy.

"We bid you welcome," said Roger extending a hand to his honoured guest.

The King clasped it firmly.

"I was saddened by the news of Robert's death. I come to greet my young vassal, even if he is only a child."

"He will learn to handle himself, I can assure you," said Roger, clearly aiming to pass a subtle message to the French monarch.

Roger nodded to the Bishop to commence the proceedings. He raised his arms as he spoke, his voice resounding around the hall.

"In the year of our Lord 1035 we are here to consecrate William, son of Robert, and his...er companion, Herleva, as Duke of Normandy, rightful successor to his father, whom God has taken to him."

Before he could continue Roger interrupted him and took centre stage to address the Barons. The Bishop could not hide his frustration. For a second time he had been prevented from conducting the ceremony.

"All of you served his father and before him his grandfather. You gave your oath to Robert that you would serve his son. Do you now give your oath to William?"

He turned and pointed to the young boy sitting on the throne. The Barons began to look at each other and gauge the reaction to Roger's question. A tall, elegantly dressed baron in his late twenties stepped forward gesturing to the other barons in the hall. Guy de Bourgogne was one of the most powerful Barons in the Duchy possessing a substantial estate at Brionne in lower Normandy. Roger knew him to be one of Duke Robert's kinsmen, but also one of his fiercest opponents.

"I ask if it is wise to place such responsibility on one so young? One of us must govern, someone with experience."

His deep voice reverberated around the hall. Roger looked at him angrily.

"Guy. Do you contest William's right and dare renounce your oath to Robert? Did he not provide you with your land enabling you to live so well off the taxes you extract?"

Count Guy turned and with a cynical smile, gestured to the assembled barons.

"That is not in dispute. But we need a strong leader. With a child as Duke our enemies in Brittany, Maine and Anjou will take it as a sign that Normandy is weak."

Roger could not disguise his frustration that there should be any opposition to the appointment of the new Duke.

"So long as all of us here today pledge allegiance to William, as rightful Duke, and promise, as true Normans, to resist any aggressor that dares to step foot in Normandy... *that* will be a sign. Who will follow me?"

Before anyone had time to respond, Roger knelt before William, who had watched and listened in silence, understanding little of the events unfolding before him.

"I, Count Roger de Beaumont, give my oath to you, William, Duke of Normandy, and pledge my loyalty to you."

One by one the barons moved forward, knelt before William and pledged alliance. Each one gave his name as they made their oath. Prince Edward, who had pondered over making any pledge, finally stepped forward and knelt before the young Duke.

"I, Prince Edward of England, give my oath to you, William, Duke of Normandy, and pledge my loyalty to you."

Roger had not taken his eyes off Guy de Bourgogne, who had been standing to one side observing the Barons as they stepped forward to give their oath. Reluctantly Guy nodded to his two faithful companions and took his vow followed by Ranulf de Briquessard and Neel de Saint Sauveur.

After all the barons had given their pledge the Bishop of Fecamp, who had been listening patiently, stepped forward and looked at Roger pleadingly. Roger nodded and the Bishop moved behind William and placed his hand on his head.

"In Nomine Patris do you swear to rule your people justly and protect the Duchy against aggression?"

William, nudged by Roger, nodded in agreement, somewhat bewildered by the ceremonial tradition.

"In the name of the Lord I hereby pronounce you, William, Duke of Normandy, the seventh of that name and may God protect you."

The Bishop held the crown above William's head not sure whether to lower it since it was too large for the young boy. Instead he offered it to William who, taking it eagerly in his hands, placed it carefully on his lap.

Most, but not all, of the Barons greeted the new Duke with cheers. Roger smiled and raised his hands for silence.

"Now we have a new Duke let us show him how good Normans feast."

A murmur of approval rose from the assembled guests as they willingly began to take their places at the long, oak tables prepared for them.

Maintaining a discreet distance from the proceedings, the monk called Lanfranc, whose presence, despite his height and colourful robes, passed unnoticed, had watched the ceremony in silence. He could not have envisaged that one day he would become one of William's closest advisors and play a crucial role in the conquest of England.

CHAPTER 7

Served by servants and maidens, scurrying between the tables, the Norman barons enjoyed a meal of venison, chicken, pork, bread, vegetables and fruit, washed down with wine and ale. William, looking tiny in comparison with the other guests, was seated at the head table between Roger and his mother. Prince Edward of England and King Henry, as honoured guests, had been placed next to Roger.

"Well Edward, how do you see your young cousin as Duke? You are now as loyal a Norman as all of us here."

Edward smiled briefly then became serious as he thought about the attempt on William's life.

"I have spent most of my life with you and seen how Robert constantly fought off his rivals. My mother brought me here to be safe from the power struggle in England. Knowing how some view his illegitimacy, I hope that my young kinsman will not have to spend his youth living in fear."

King Henry was listening. "As his overlord, he can rely on me."

Roger was looking down at William still tightly clasping his crown. He spoke quietly to his guests.

"The crown may not fit....yet. But it will."

Seated at the end of one of the tables, too far away to have overheard Edward's remarks, Guy de Bourgogne, Ranulf de Briquessard, and Neel de Saint Sauveur, were talking quietly amongst themselves clearly resentful about serving the new Duke of Normandy, whom they considered was not fit to rule over them. They had grown up together and formed part of the Normandy establishment. With Guy, master of the region around Brionne and Ranulf and Neel respectively Viscounts of the Bessin and Cotentin regions, the trio, formed a powerful alliance.

"We failed once to rid Normandy of William. We are not going to allow this bastard to stand in our way now?" Guy sat clenching his fist.

The others nodded in agreement.

"Let us not express our thoughts too loud," whispered Ranulf.

Neel moved his face closer to his companions.

"For power to pass into our hands, we cannot ignore those loyal to William. His mother has many kinsmen who pledged allegiance to him. It is not certain that we can persuade them to submit to our terms."

Guy nodded at both of them. "If they do not, they will bear the consequences. We also gave our vow to William. But there are many, including Robert's own kinsmen, who do not accept a Duke born out of wedlock. We will deal with William in our own way."

Not wishing to draw attention to themselves the three barons sat back and continued eating and drinking, engaging in polite conversation with the other nobles. Robert's death was hardly something to celebrate and the atmosphere was subdued.

From time to time Roger glanced up at the gallery. Standing at regular intervals in the shadows hidden by heavy curtains were loyal men at arms he had posted to keep a watchful eye on events. Their discreet presence went unnoticed by the guests.

The banquet drew to a close. Separately or in small groups the barons drifted away from the great hall to collect their horses and return to their estates, their place taken by servants, busy emptying the tables and cleaning the floor. After bidding farewell to the last visitors, Roger, Arlette and William retired together to an antechamber of the castle. Roger appeared concerned and once the door closed behind them, began to stalk around the room, his hands clasped behind his back. He stopped by the window and looked out. After a moment's silence he turned to William's mother.

"You saw that many of the Barons present here today are loyal but some, even amongst our own kinsmen, cannot be trusted. For the future of Normandy the young Duke must be trained to become a War Lord, and one day, to rule."

Arlette was taken back by Roger's comment and clasped William to her.

"I know your experience will be of great help in teaching him the ways of war but to rule he must also become learned..."

Interrupting, William blurted out.

"I want to learn to ride like my father."

Arlette patted him on the head.

"Of course you will, all in good time."

Roger nodded, appreciating Arlette's commonsense.

"Then I suggest we arrange for your kinsmen to take him into the sanctuary of the church. He will be safe there. He will learn to read and write and become a true Christian."

Arlette smiled and nodded in agreement as they both looked down at the young Duke. She knew she would be able to rely on the church to look after her son.

CHAPTER 8

And so the young Duke William, at the age of eight, was sent to Jumieges, the monastery some 100 kilometres from Falaise. Following in the footsteps of his kinsman, Prince Edward, he was placed in the care of monks and scholars and taught the basic elements of writing and reading. He shared their prayers and listened to their teachings as they instilled in him the ways of a true Christian. As time passed, William learnt to appreciate the silence of the monastery. He joined other boys of his age, earning their friendship, learning to play games and sharing the domestic chores of clearing tables, making beds and cleaning dormitories, always under the watchful eyes of the monks.

One evening after prayers and supper a monk was seated at the end of the hall, quietly reading at his desk. There was the barely audible murmur of conversation coming from the dormitories, but nothing to disturb him. Suddenly the silence was broken by shouts and banging. The monk hastily put down his book and hurried down the corridor to find where the noise was coming from. He opened the door to the dormitory to see two boys writhing about on the floor while others were jumping up and down on beds screaming their encouragement.

"Stop. Enough of that, back to your beds," shouted the monk pushing his way in and pulling the two boys apart.

The next morning, with the sun rising early heralding the first signs of spring, William was walking with the Abbot in the cloister. The Abbot had spent a lifetime in the austere environment of the church and had been a faithful servant to William's father. But at sixty-one his health was failing and he could only walk at a slow pace stopping from time to time to rest. He looked down at the young boy.

"What happened last night?"

William's head dropped and he looked at the ground sheepishly.

"The others called me a... a bastard."

"Ah, I see," said the Abbot.

William often found solace listening to the Abbot's gentle and soothing voice.

"You know that is something you are going to have to live with. You are different from the others. The union of your father and mother was not according to the Christian church. Your enemies will use it to discredit you but they are only words. You must learn to respond in the same way. Words can sometimes be a more powerful weapon than the sword. You are a Duke and must act as a leader as well as a Christian."

"Will I be as strong as my father?" enquired William.

"You will be as strong as you want to be. But in this house it is God who is all powerful."

"But who is God? You pray to him, you teach me the ways of God, yet I have not seen him."

They continued to stroll around the cloister and as they reached a corner of the cloister William stopped and glanced up at the wall. Looking down at him was a wooden statue of the Christ on the cross. William took his medallion and looked at the tiny, engraved crucifix.

The Abbott smiled.

"God is both here and everywhere in spirit. We carry out his wishes and teach others to follow the righteous path."

"Will he fight my enemies?" asked William, still handling his medallion.

The Abbott placed his arm on William's shoulder and sat down on the stone base of a pillar. "Let me rest a while, William."

He looked at the young boy, now ten years old and growing up fast.

"No. God does not fight. He has no enemies. He preaches peace and he will help you overcome adversity. Learn God's ways and you will understand that you can never rule by the sword alone. You need wisdom and knowledge. Knowledge comes from your studies, and with knowledge comes wisdom. A true leader needs wisdom to make decisions, which are often difficult and he must also learn humility to take heed of the advice of others when it is well founded. He has to learn to be just and magnanimous with all people and sometimes, in exercising justice, even to his enemies."

William looked lost. "Magmininus?"

The Abbot smiled again wagging his finger. "Mag-nan-imous. It means to be forgiving; as God forgives even if someone calls you a bastard."

As they continued to stroll slowly around the grounds, a servant waiting with two horses caught the Abbot's attention.

"Ah, Osbern. It is time for your riding lesson. He will take you to Vaudreuil for the night. You can return tomorrow"

Osbern de Crepon was a loyal servant to William's parents and had been charged with the task of protecting him. At twenty-five he was tall, physically strong, a fine rider and enjoyed being able to teach William the art of horsemanship. William ran excitedly towards Osbern and grabbed the reins of one of the horses. He leapt into the saddle and turned his horse to ride off, his prowess gaining the admiration of the Abbott, who shook his head and sighed anxiously as he watched the reckless youngster gallop away. The Abbott gestured to Osbern to follow. After politely taking his leave it took all his skill to chase after William as he careered off towards the forest.

For more than two hours Osbern gave one of his regular lessons in the art of horsemanship to his young prodigy before it was time to accompany William to the castle at Le Vaudreuil to spend the night. Osbern had noticed the clouds gathering menacingly while William had been manoeuvring his horse, jumping over obstacles, making turns and riding in a circle without using the reins.

"Master, we need to begin our journey to the castle. There is a storm approaching."

"I will race you back Osbern, and beat you."

"You can try, master."

William sank his heels into his horse's flank and raced off. Osbern, caught unawares, had difficulty in catching him. They galloped through the Normandy countryside following the course of the river Seine, stopping only to rest for a short break and partake of some food and drink that Osbern had brought with him. William liked to show how fast he could ride and at one point they almost collided with a group of peasants on their way home from the fields, almost causing their wagon to topple over. In the process of avoiding them they created a cloud of dust that left the peasants coughing and cursing at the two horsemen as they disappeared over a hill.

By the time they reached the gates of Le Vaudreuil it was dusk. They were so exhausted that they had not noticed the two horsemen that had been following them at a distance for the last few kilometres. As they climbed the steps to William's bedchamber reflecting on their journey, the riders were entering the castle and wasted little time to unsaddle and tether their mounts in the stables.

Inside the chamber Osbern lit a candle and they began to take off their dusty clothes.

"One day I will be able to beat you."

"Master, I do not doubt it. I can mount and handle a horse as well as anyone but I have watched you and can tell that you will be a match for any horseman. Now, we must sleep."

They both retired to their beds and lay down, pulling the covers over them. Osbern cupped his hand around the flame and blew it out. Flashes of lightening lit up the room as the sound of thunder crashed above the castle and the wind and rain lashed outside. Disturbed by the storm, William was only half asleep when he heard a sound. He glanced towards the door and saw it creak open. In the darkness he could make out two figures creeping into the room. William silently slid out of the covers and under his bed. Osbern, hearing footsteps, sat up and seeing two figures before him instantly reached for his sword. He cried out for help as the two men rushed forward, their knives raised. They plunged their daggers into Osbern, then glanced around the room. They approached William's empty bed before a sound outside caused them to panic. They ran out leaving the door open. After what seemed like several minutes two men burst in, their swords raised. One went immediately to Osbern who was groaning in pain, trying hopelessly to raise himself from the bed.

"Osbern, you are hurt! As he touched him he saw blood seeping through his nightdress. "Oh Seigneur! Did you see who it was?"

Osbern shook his head, tried to speak then fell back to the floor. He did not move again. In the darkness William had recognised the man's voice and began to crawl out from under the bed. Hearing the sound the men turned towards the bed, swords raised.

"William, you are safe, thank God," said the taller of the two men. Walter and Osbert, were his uncles, brothers of his mother. Roger had taken the precaution of asking Arlette's trusted kinsmen to watch over the young Duke. They were both young men in their mid twenties of medium build, with long, blond hair and dressed in the attire of peasants.

"Get dressed quickly," urged Walter. "We must leave."

Osbert went to the door and looked outside. "There is nobody about."

"Find your way to the north tower and bring horses. We will meet you there."

As Osbert disappeared William stood stunned, staring at Osbern's bloodstained body. Before he had time to express any feelings, Walter took his hand and ushered him out of the room. He led him, frightened, along a corridor. Hearing voices they hid behind a wall. Walter had his hand covering William's mouth. Two soldiers passed, their torches throwing ghostly shadows on the walls. They were joined by a third soldier.

"Is it done yet?"

"He is not in his room."

"What! Then find him. We cannot let him escape or we risk our own lives."

The sound of their heavy footsteps on the stone floor grew fainter. Walter waited until there was total silence, then whispered to William. "This way."

They moved cautiously to another stairwell and climbed to the turret. The storm was still at its height with another crash of thunder followed almost immediately by flashes of lightning, which lit up the night sky.

Walter, covering his head to protect himself from the drenching rain, threw a rope over the side and attached it to a steel ring projecting from the wall of the ramparts. Pulling hard on the rope to check that it was secure, he beckoned William to take it. Clutching the rope as tightly as he could, with Walter's help, William slid over the side, his feet dangling in space. Walter followed and one at a time they lowered themselves. They were getting soaked and swayed in the wind. Osbert, waiting with horses, had seen the rope swinging by the wall and grabbed it to keep it taught.

"I had to get past two guards to reach our horses," he said when both Walter and William were safely on the ground.

Walter covered himself and William with his cloak.

"You go to Falaise and warn Roger. We will not make it to the castle tonight. I will take William to father's cottage. We shall be safe there."

Walter lifted William onto his horse and they rode off into the night still being drenched by the heavy rain. Reaching a clearing in the forest they parted company.

Osbert headed towards Falaise while Walter and William took to the path by the river, which he thought would be safer. At one point Walter stopped. Despite the swaying of the trees in the wind he thought he had heard the sound of horses.

"I hear something. This is no time to find out if they are friend or foe. Better to be cautious."

He guided his horse off the path, down an embankment towards a cluster of trees. They watched in silence as a group of knights, unrecognisable in the darkness, galloped past. When all was silent and it seemed safe again they continued their journey. Sometime later, weary and drenched to the skin, they reached a cottage on the banks of the river.

Inside the simple, timber cottage with its thatched roof, his beard and lined features making him look older than his years, Fulbert was seated dozing by the fire when he was awoken by a loud knock outside. He picked up a wooden club and went to the door. The rain and wind was pounding the roof.

"Who calls at this late hour?"

"Walter and young William."

The man laid down his club and unbolted the door, holding it tight against the wind. Once Walter and William were safely inside he forced the door shut with a bang and bolted it. He took William in his arms.

Arlette's father had been a tanner to the court at Falaise and had been both surprised and delighted when the Duke fell in love with his daughter, and taken her for his companion. Although it had allowed him to finally escape the routine of rising before dawn and toiling away in the tannery, he was resentful that the Duke had never taken Christian vows and left William to bear the stigma of being an illegitimate child. Walter had often brought William to the cottage to spend time with his grandfather at his sister's request. Now getting on for sixty years old, physically weak from the years spent hunched over his bench in the workshop, he looked down at the wet, shivering child standing before him.

"What brings you here in the darkness of night? Where is your mother?"

Walter intervened. "It has been a rough night. Let William sleep. I will tell you what happened."

Fulbert prepared a bed while Walter took off William's wet clothes hanging them to dry by the fire. Despite the late hour, a bowl of soup and bread was quickly prepared. After the exhausted William lay down to sleep the two men sat eating and drinking in front of the fire. Shadows flickered onto their faces as Walter explained to his father everything that had happened that night. William's grandfather listened shocked, turning from time to time towards William as if to reassure himself that he was safe.

The next morning was calm. The storm had passed. Raindrops on the grass and reeds lining the banks of the river glistened in the morning sunlight. The only sounds were the croaking of frogs, chirping of birds and ripple of water as the river flowed smoothly through the valley towards the sea.

Walter gave his horse a rub down and then threw on the saddle making sure the straps were tied, while William and Fulbert sat on the porch watching. When he was ready Walter turned to his father.

"Thank you for giving us shelter but we need to reach Falaise as soon as possible. I won't return to Jumieges today. I only hope we don't run into any of those assailants responsible for last night."

Fulbert took William in his arms and gave him a hug.

"My boy, you are already too big for me to pick you up. When you come back we can go fishing together. What do you say?"

William nodded. "I would like that."

"May God be with you."

Walter helped William up into the saddle in front of him. William waved to his grandfather as Walter spun the horse round and headed towards the river, following its course as it meandered its way through the Normandy countryside towards Falaise. Standing by the door of the cottage, Fulbert stood watching them until the trees swallowed them up.

CHAPTER 9

Count Roger was in a rage. Prince Edward and Robert of Jumieges said nothing as they stood watching him stride up and down the great hall of Falaise castle. Arlette just sat motionless not wishing to think about what had happened. Robert broke the silence.

"How long must we endure these attacks on William?"

"This is what I feared most for my young cousin," added Edward.

"Is it not time you took matters into our own hands?" enquired Robert, trying to be helpful. "You must know who is behind these attacks."

Yes, but I don't want to risk a civil war in Normandy or engage in conflict with Brittany and France while the Duke is not yet of age. We must bide our time."

Arlette was becoming angry. "Is that all you think about, war?"

"Not if it can be avoided," replied Roger curtly. "But we must consider William's future."

"With traitors everywhere perhaps it would be wise to abandon your hunting trip?" suggested Robert. Edward glanced at Roger.

"Absolutely not," retorted Roger. "I will not be seen to cower before anybody. We will show them how we react to their treachery."

Roger gestured to Edward.

"Edward has been waiting for this hunt. If he leaves for England, it may be the last time we hunt together and this time we will take William with us."

"What! Is that wise? exclaimed Arlette. "The Abbott expects him at Jumieges."

"He will be safer in our company."

"Then you do not intend to search for the assassins?" queried Edward.

Roger looked at him.

"We know who they are. But first William must be protected. Thank God Arlette's kinsmen are loyal. They can be trusted until he is old enough to look after himself."

Roger thumped his fist on the table.

"I promise you the time will come."

Hunting was not something any medieval baron worth his salt would pass up. Early the following morning Roger, with Prince Edward by his side, rode out of the castle at the head of a small contingent. They were accompanied by several barons whose loyalty was unquestionable, servants in a horse-driven wagon, and at the rear, more household staff on foot with hounds and falcons. William rode between Walter and Osbert, who never left his side.

Their route took them across rolling green hills and woodland. Reaching a river not far from the castle, they followed its path until they came to a clearing in the forest at a point where the river changed its course.

"This is as good a place to rest as any," announced Roger, signalling to the entourage to halt. The knights dismounted leaving their horses in the care of the servants who then proceeded to unload sacks carrying provisions from the wagon. Everyone found somewhere to sit and food and wine were handed round. Roger, seated on the trunk of a fallen tree, took his knife, sliced off a chunk of meat and handed a piece to Edward.

"Here, eat this. While those Vikings, Saxons and Celts kill each other in England, stay with us. After all you have Norman blood in your veins. You hunt so well."

The group all laughed. Edward, in between bites, looked up and smiled.

"I thank you. The situation in England is changing. The Viking threat still exists in Northumbria but the Saxons control

the south. Earl Godwin is the most powerful Saxon in the Kingdom and has promised me his support. Now my half brother,
Hardicanute, is dead the time is propitious for me to return and
claim the throne."

As Edward was about to tuck into some meat he heard a
sound coming from behind some bushes.

"A boar! This one's mine."

Edward set down his food, got to his feet and went to the
wagon where he picked up a bow and a quiver. He extracted an
arrow and carefully placed it in the bow. Raising it to his eye
ready to take aim, he moved stealthily towards the bushes.
Suddenly with a crashing sound, a large, angry, black animal, its
eyes glowing and snorting loudly came charging out of the
undergrowth towards him. Edward moved aside fast, allowing
the boar to charge towards the seated knights who dropped their
food and scattered. One knight standing by the river bank
slipped and fell backwards into the water with a loud splash as
the boar passed. Another jumped in to save himself. Edward
meanwhile had followed the boar's movements. It pulled up by
the water's edge turned and faced the hounds which had closed
in on the animal, barking noisily. As it stood its ground, grunt-
ing and eyeing the hounds, considering which way to move,
Edward carefully pulled back the bowstring taking aim before
releasing an arrow, which sped accurately into the Boar's side.
The boar's legs gave way under him and, as he tried to recover,
a second arrow hit his body close to the heart and the boar
toppled over, dead. Regaining his composure, after checking that
the animal was indeed dead, Roger slapped Edward on the back.

"Your aim is excellent. We will enjoy a feast before you
begin your journey."

The other barons picked themselves up and gathered their
belongings, while the knights who had fallen into the water
were drying themselves, all in good humour. William excited by
the unforeseen action approached the carcass and slowly
extracted the two arrows. He carried them over to where
Edward was seated and handed them to him.

"Keep them as a souvenir, from me." said Edward, patting him on the head.

William smiled and carefully placed them in the sack on his back. Then he watched as the servants heaved the dead boar into the wagon.

That night the banqueting hall was crowded and noisy. As was the custom, Roger, Arlette, William and their honoured guest, Edward, were seated at the main table. Robert of Jumieges had been offered a place next to Edward. Roger stood up and raised his hand. The conversation ceased.

"I propose a toast to Edward. He has turned down all my attempts to persuade him to stay with us. He thinks now of England and his return to take the crown. We wish him a safe journey."

Edward stood up and raised his goblet.

"I have spent my youth here. I will never forget the Abbey of Jumieges. Although born in England I now consider myself a Norman."

Cheers echoed around the room.

"And as a Norman I pledge to you a loyal and lasting friendship. But I am also a Saxon and a sense of duty calls for me to accept the responsibility of ruling my country, England. Fortunately, I will have the benefit of the advice and friendship of Robert, who will be accompanying me. His counsel will be invaluable."

Edward turned to Robert, placing his hand on his shoulder.

"I take my leave with a heavy heart."

Edward did not forget William and placing his hand on his shoulder raised his goblet. "Rule wisely my young kinsman. We will surely meet again."

Everyone rose to their feet and raised their goblets. They had momentarily ignored the young Duke. Throughout the feast, William had remained seated just watching and listening but while he was becoming accustomed to being a spectator at such events, little escaped his attention and he was learning.

CHAPTER 10

The Saxon Chronicles:
"This year (1043) was Edward consecrated king at Winchester
early on Easter day with much pomp. Then was Easter on the
third day before the nones of April. Archbishop Edsy conse-
crated him and before all people well admonished him."

Edward arrived in England to take the crown. King Hardicanute, his Viking kinsman, had died suddenly at Lambeth.
During a bout of drinking he toppled over and, to the surprise
of his companions, breathed no more. Hardicanute had been
King for just two years succeeding his father, King Cnut, and
then his elder half brother.

Edward's father, King Aethelred had died in 1016, while Edward was growing up in Normandy. His mother Emma of
Normandy had returned to England and became betrothed to
the new King, Cnut. She bore him a son named Hardicanute.
Thus Cnut became Edward's stepfather and Hardicanute his
stepbrother. Of all the potential pretenders in Norway, Denmark and England, Edward's right to accede to the throne
could not be refuted. Arriving at the Palace of Winchester, he
was surprised to see the reception hall crowded with Saxon
nobility keen to see their new King. To one side stood a
group of Saxons in colourful robes. They were the members
of the Witan, the body of sixty nobles and clergymen who
presided over affairs of state and of law. The last time the
elders had seen Edward he was just a child and anyone
not yet thirty had only heard of the young prince exiled in
Normandy.

"So at last we are going to meet our new King." said an Earl
standing next to Earl Godwin, considered to be one of the most
powerful Saxon landowners.

"Let's hope he lasts longer than his predecessor," replied Godwin ironically.

As Earl Godwin stepped forward to greet the prince from Normandy, everyone was asking himself who was the young abbot accompanying Edward.

"I am Godwin of Wessex."

Edward looked at the man facing him. "I thought as much."

"At last we welcome your return to England, Edward. Your rightful place as King is assured and we pledge our loyalty to you."

Godwin's voice boomed around the hall. He was in his early forties and of medium height but his tunic could not hide the well built body with muscular arms. His blond hair was long and his weathered face, almost hidden by a large moustache and beard, bore the scars of battle.

"It's been a long time," replied Edward looking around at the Saxon nobility.

"I see you have not returned alone," said Godwin.

"Oh!" exclaimed Edward apologetically. "Let me introduce you to my trusted friend Robert Champart of Jumieges. He will be advising me on matters of the church."

As Edward beckoned Robert to step forward, Godwin glanced around at his Saxon friends and the buzz of conversation rose up from the hall.

"You must take the crown before your Viking cousins have second thoughts. You have the support of members of the Witan," reassured Godwin turning towards the Saxon nobles."

"I will need time to adjust," said Edward.

"Don't take too long." There was almost a hint of warning in Godwin's voice.

"What happened to my brother Alfred," enquired Edward. It was a leading question directed personally at Earl Godwin.

"We have not elucidated the crime," mumbled Godwin trying to sound convincing, "It was a shock to us all. Rest assured we will find the assassins."

Edward nodded unconvinced but before he could pursue the matter Godwin intervened, changing the subject and beckoning three young people to step closer.

"Edward, meet my sons, Harold and Tostig, and my daughter Edith.

Godwin's hand lingered on Harold's shoulder. In his late teens, Harold was tall and muscular, like his father, with piercing blue eyes and a thick moustache. His long blond hair reached down to his shoulders. Like all his brothers he had been raised in conventional fashion. Peasants had taught him the rudimentary skills to hunt and fish and from childhood he had learnt to appreciate and respect animals and hunting birds. It had become second nature for him to handle horses and raise the hounds and falcons on his father's estates. Above all he had learnt from his father that land meant power; the larger the landholdings the more power wielded. And Godwin had acquired more than his fair share of land in southern England. Harold was the son being groomed to succeed Godwin despite the growing resentment of Tostig, who found it difficult to conceal his jealous nature. He had grown up with a sentiment of being ignored by his father.

"And this is Edith."

Godwin beckoned his daughter to step closer then whispered in Edward's ear. "She is almost of age to wed. Would she not make a fine Queen?"

Edward's eyebrows rose as he glanced at the rather plain child who smiled back shyly. Having made his point, Godwin's thoughts moved on to more pressing matters.

"Now it is time to meet members of the Witan. They will wish to discuss affairs of state and prepare your coronation."

As Godwin gestured towards the Saxon nobles, Robert put his head close to Edward and spoke softly.

"I do not think the Saxons appreciate my presence here."

"If I am to be King, I decide who shall advise me," murmured Edward. "Come let's not keep the dignitaries waiting."

And so it was that with the backing of the Witan and all the people that Edward, the Prince, more Norman than Saxon, was duly crowned King of England at Winchester on Easter day 1043.

CHAPTER 11

Meanwhile, in Normandy William was growing up. The early part of his teenage years had been divided between monasteries, castles and Norman villages, where he was raised and protected by peasants loyal to his mother. The majority of the Norman people had learnt to respect and admire the young man who was their Duke.

At fourteen he was already tall and strong for his age. Thanks to the Abbots and with Roger's guiding hand he was rapidly learning what it required to be a leader; he was mature beyond his years. But the threat from the rebel Barons who opposed him had never abated. Roger had been right about his father's kinsmen. Many Norman Barons could not be trusted and it was no secret that their one aim was to rid the Duchy of the bastard child. Roger had never forgotten the promise he had given to Arlette many years before, after they had received the news of Duke Robert's death. It was now time, he thought, for William to be taught how to defend himself, time to become a War Lord.

During one of their hunting expeditions, Roger had taken William to the forest near Falaise. As usual, they were accompanied by mounted bodyguards because the risk to the young Duke had not diminished. Towards midday they reached a clearing in the forest, where they dismounted and sat down to rest. After feasting, Roger got to his feet and walked to his horse. He extracted a large sword from the scabbard and struck it forcefully into the ground.

"You already ride like a knight. I once promised your mother I would teach you to handle a sword. Now take it."

William stood up, strolled towards the sword and placed both hands around the hilt. Pulling hard, he slowly lifted the heavy, steel weapon, almost as big as he was, and began to make sweeping passes with both hands. Roger watched him, grinning.

"This was your father's sword. It is now yours. Learn from me and it will serve you well."

Roger extracted his own sword from its scabbard and pointed it at the teenager standing before him. The other knights looked on amused as William exchanged blows gently with his uncle who offered advice.

"Keep your legs apart and balanced, don't raise your arm too high. No. No. Try again. Good. Again. Now left, cut across, defend yourself."

They exchanged blows slowly, the clashing of steel ringing through the trees. William attempted an ambitious lunge forward but Roger parried the blow and knocked William's sword out of his hands while bringing his own sword up against William's body.

"You see what happens. Now try again."

William looked annoyed as he picked up the fallen sword. Roger prodded his sword towards William's chest.

"One more thing. You will always confront danger. But never be afraid. Let me tell you about Courage and Fear."

Stabbing his sword into the ground he put his arm around William's shoulders, looking closely at him as he told him the story his own father had passed down to him.

"The Courage stands before the gates of the castle of The Fear. The Courage asks. "Is anyone there?" The Fear answers. "The Fear." Undeterred, the Courage pushes open the gates and enters. But there is no one there."

"Remember that," Roger said smiling as he pinched William on the cheek, leaving him with a rather bemused expression on his young face.

CHAPTER 12

It was a dark, stormy night in Bayeux. The villagers had heard riders passing by their cottages but remained inside their homes. At the sound of another horse's hooves splashing through the muddy ground, one curious peasant peered out from the door of his humble abode to see what was happening. In the darkness he could make out a lone horseman, unrecognisable in his cloak and hood, riding slowly towards the priory. He shrugged his shoulders and shut the door, taking care to bolt it. The horseman passed through the priory gates into the grounds and dismounted. A door opened in the side wall of the building and a figure appeared holding a torch that projected a shaft of light flickering across the yard, illuminating the porch. Removing his hood, the man stepped out of the shadows revealing a face with drawn features, a thin mouth and a pair of cold eyes staring towards the light as it beckoned him towards it.

"Welcome, Hamon, come in. The others are here."

Ranulf de Briquessard was standing by the porch with his hand outstretched. The visitor took it firmly and entered. Ranulf shut the door behind him as Count Hamon de Creully strode across to the fire to dry himself. He nodded to the five other men present. Seated at the table, Guy de Bourgogne, Count Grimoult de Plessis, Raoul Taisson, William Talvas, Lord of Belleme, and Viscount Neel, bowed their heads in return. The men were kinsmen, descendants of Duke Richard 1 and Richard 11. All of them, except the young Raoul Taisson, still only in his early twenties, were now in their thirties and had never given up their ambition to rule the Duchy. Known as the "Richardists," they had infiltrated the corridors of power undertaking covert operations against Duke Robert whenever the opportunity arose. His untimely death during his pilgrimage to the Holy Land had left Normandy in the hands of a child and given them the chance for which they had been waiting. For years, they had been gathering support amongst the barons of lower Normandy. With a bastard seated on the throne of the Duchy, they were more confident than ever before that others would rally to their cause.

With their goblets filled with wine, the seven men sat, drank and talked of the matter that had brought them together. Guy of Bourgogne placed his goblet on the table.

"Gentlemen, our attempts so far to rid Normandy of this bastard Duke have failed. It has been six years and I fear time is running out."

"There is no doubt that as he grows older he becomes stronger," uttered Neel.

"To have journeyed here on such a foul night shows our resolve," added Ranulf, earning the consensus of all around the table.

Each in turn put forward his views.

"There are many who do not want that bastard to rule the Duchy," said Hamon.

Grimault nodded. "Even the Pope has misgivings."

"So long as William rules, we remain vulnerable to threats from France, Anjou and Brittany," added William Talvas.

"Then our thoughts must be turned into deeds," reaffirmed Guy, looking at his companions.

For over an hour they plotted and schemed until their minds were forged as one. When they had drunk enough and were ready to leave they knew the time had come to make a decision from which there would be no turning back.

Raoul Taisson had listened attentively to his companions' arguments. He nodded approvingly to show support, but deep down he was not entirely convinced.

"Do we give our pledge?"

Count Hamon raised his eyes and looked around at his companions while lifting his goblet. A unanimous "Aye" rang out, and the sound of silver goblets clinking together reverberated around the hall.

PART II

CHAPTER 13

In Normandy the next four years were turbulent times as the rebel Barons pursued their campaign against William's reign. However, whatever cunning plot they hatched to eliminate the young Duke, whether through luck or courage, he survived; destiny was on his side. The Duke was growing in confidence and stature and by the time he reached nineteen he was both physically strong and mature enough to stand his own ground. The tide had turned and the barons who had previously dared to oppose him now feared the young Duke of Normandy. He was an audacious warrior whose daring exploits had made him a feared opponent and he possessed an undeniable physical presence.

Those who had been tempted to call him a bastard, no longer expressed themselves aloud and never to his face. While not handsome he was tall and muscular, with rugged features and clear blue eyes. His blond hair was now closely cropped with a fringe covering his forehead and he had grown a moustache.

The Normandy countryside possessed an abundance of wildlife and in pure Norman tradition the young Duke had become an avid huntsman. While enjoying an expedition in the Valognes forest he engaged in another bout of fencing with Roger to the amusement of the other barons and servants who had accompanied them. They had witnessed William grow into a strong young man, a skilled horseman and now an expert swordsman. After several minutes exchanging blows William parried an attack and lunged forward, forcing his uncle's sword downwards and twisting his arm backwards so that he had to let go of his weapon, which clattered to the ground. Roger reached down to retrieve his sword and sat down to rest. He glanced up at William, who now towered over him.

"Enough, you are tiring me. I am getting too old for this. Sit down with me."

William thrust his sword into the ground and taking a jug of wine sat down next to his loyal kinsman.

"You don't need me to fight your enemies. You have learnt well. Rarely have I seen anyone so strong."

"I have followed your advice these last years."

"You are a formidable opponent, William. You ride and wield a sword better than anyone. But will you be a great leader?"

"I will rule Normandy as you have taught me to rule."

"And, I hope, follow the Abbot's advice."

"What advice?"

"That you are different from the others…"

William cut Roger short.

"If you mean I was born a bastard, I know."

"Vengeance is not a virtue. Just try to be a good Christian."

"I shall," replied William, gulping down some wine. "So long as nobody reminds me of my origin to my face." Wiping his mouth, he helped himself to some meat.

Roger sighed but said nothing. Had he failed his young prodigy? While his guiding had transformed William into a powerful warrior and a leader, his illegitimacy still represented a psychological hurdle to overcome. He raised himself to his feet and changed the subject.

"It is a pity your cousin Edward had to return to England. He would have enjoyed this day but he must fulfil his duties as King. In a few years it will be your mission to go to England and remind Edward of his pledge to you and to Normandy."

"Perhaps… once the Duchy is united," said William.

Roger looked towards the sky. "It is past midday, I have hunted enough this day. It is time to return to Falaise."

"You go," said William. "Have you forgotten, I must go to Valognes? I cannot leave without paying my respects to Viscounts Bessin and Cotentin. They are waiting at the Monastery."

Roger looked concerned.

"Is it wise to go alone? I cannot vouch for their loyalty."

William was acutely aware of the attempts on his life.

"Don't worry. I can handle myself and anyway, Goles will accompany me."

William gestured to a dwarf who was taking care of the horses. Goles was already twenty-two but looked much younger. Born with a physical defect, there had been few opportunities open to him except to become a court jester. But he also had an affinity towards animals. He spent as much time as possible with the hounds and horses and had been delighted when offered the chance to look after the knights' horses in the castle.

William and Goles climbed into their saddles and watched as Roger and the hunting party gathered their belongings and rode off towards Falaise. Then they turned their horses and headed off in the opposite direction, making their way through the forest to the monastery at Valognes. It would be a journey that would determine the future of Normandy.

Valognes was in the Cotentin peninsula and was one of Roger's favourite forests. Although far from Falaise, it was only a short distance from where they had been hunting. The Viscounts of Bessin and Cotentin had given their consent to the building of the Monastery to enable the church to have a presence in one of Normandy's more isolated regions. Located in a clearing in the forest, the monastery had the appearance of a castle, rather than a house of God. Behind the turreted high walls, the living quarters and prayer rooms were built around a square with the single entrance through a gated arch opening into a courtyard, which in turn led to a central cloister. On one side of the court-yard were the stables. The sun was still high in the sky when William and Goles rode through the unguarded gate into the courtyard to be greeted by their two hosts who had been advised of their arrival.

"Welcome to Valognes, Sire," said Viscount Neel. "We have prepared a feast for you. But first you might like to wash and rest."

"We can only offer you the monk's chambers. They are spartan but comfortable," added Viscount Ranulf. "As you can imagine."

As Goles led the horses away, William was escorted to the guest quarters inside. He had noticed several knights watching his movements from a corner of the courtyard. Monks were going about their business. William was led through the cloister to the first floor where a servant unlocked a plain wooden door and invited William to enter. William had to lower his head as he followed the servant into the room. It was laid out for a monk and was extremely bare, as he had been warned. Pushed up against one wall was a single wooden framed bed with a thin mattress. In one corner there was an old wooden closet, and by the window there was a small table on which stood a basin and jug. The servant left William alone shutting the door behind him. William went to the window and saw that they overlooked gardens. He then checked the door lifting the catch. It was not locked. He looked outside but the corridor was empty. Closing the door quietly he slid the bolt into place, went to the table, filled the basin with water from the jug, laid his sword on the bed and began to take off his outer garments.

Inside the stables Goles had unsaddled and tethered the horse, gave it a rub down, and was carefully cleaning the mud from its hooves when he heard voices. He stopped what he was doing and kept low and silent behind the wooden barriers of the stall. Two knights had entered the stables and were talking quietly, but loud enough for Goles to hear their conversation.

"Here, take this sword," said one of the men. Goles tried to peer between the cracks in the planks. He could make out two men picking up weapons, which had been stacked in a corner.

"You know which room he is in. The Viscounts will pay us well."

Goles put his hand over his mouth in shock and waited until the men had gone. Certain he was alone again, he discarded the cloth and made his way to the rear stable door. After looking outside to make sure there was nobody in sight, he scurried across the courtyard into the cloister and made his way up the steps. William was washing in his room when he heard a noise outside as if someone was trying to force the door. He instinctively went for his sword, moved towards the door and slid back the bolt. With his arm raised he pulled the door open. As Goles entered he lowered his sword sliding it back into its scabbard and shut the door behind him. Goles was out of breath and his voice hardly audible.

"Sire, you cannot stay here. I was in the stables and overhead soldiers talking about a plot to kill you."

"Are you certain?" William looked at him in disbelief. "I know the Viscounts have never looked too favourably on me, but to plot against me here. I am indebted to you. Now we must escape from this place."

Goles grinned mischievously. "We? I am not coming with you. Sire. No one saw me come to warn you. I will stay here. But I know a secret passage which leads to the garden beyond the walls."

"But I cannot leave on foot."

"That's not a problem. No one questions me with animals. I will guide you to the passage and then bring your horse to the garden."

William looked around.

"I cannot leave in these clothes."

He pulled opened the closet, the door almost falling off its hinges. Inside hung a few monk's garments. He took them out and spread them on the bed. Sorting through the collection, he chose a monk's black habit, held it up and put it on over his clothes, tying the cord around his waist and covering his head with the hood.

"This will help get past the guards."

Goles nodded his approval then carefully opened the door and looked up and down the hallway. It was empty. He beckoned William to follow. They slowly walked along the terrace overlooking the cloister. There were several monks seated below, meditating. Descending the stone steps they noticed two guards standing by a door at the end of the corridor. Goles pointed to the entrance of the cloister. William, walking slowly as if in prayer, crossed the hall and sidled out into the cloister. The guards looked up but took no notice of a monk shuffling along the corridor. Once across the cloister, after entering another hallway, Goles stopped by a curtain. He pulled it to expose a door partially hidden behind a pillar. Looking around to make sure they were not being watched, William turned the handle and the door opened inwards. There were stone steps leading down into what seemed like a black hole.

"Go!" said Goles looking around worried in case someone might see them. "I will meet you at the other end."

William had hardly begun to make his way down when Goles closed the door and the curtain behind him leaving him in total darkness. With no other choice but to move forward, William slowly descended the steps one at a time until his feet touched the bottom. He cursed as he banged his head on the roof. The air was stale. Bending down, he moved cautiously along the dark, narrow passage. From the feel of the supports William guessed the tunnel was propped up by timbers. He edged slowly forward until he felt a breeze caressing his cheeks. He could make out a speck of light in the distance, which grew larger as he moved towards it. Reaching the opening, he gently pulled back the branches that covered the entrance and breathed in the fresh air. He peered outside. He could see an open field bounded by trees about one hundred metres away. He realized he would be exposed until he reached the safety of the forest. It was quiet. William waited anxiously as time passed staying hidden until he heard the sound of a horse. After what seemed like several minutes Goles's head appeared through the bushes.

"Sire, it is safe. You can come out."

William removed the monk's habit, discarded it and clambered out looking around to make sure they were still alone. He checked that his sword was in its scabbard, tightened the straps of the saddle and prepared to mount. Once in the saddle William took his shield, slotted his bow and quiver behind him and, leaning down, placed his hand on Goles's shoulder.

"I will not forget your loyalty."

"Go quickly, Sire."

With that, Goles disappeared into the hole. William wondered if Goles would face any danger for helping him escape, but he could only promise himself that if anything ever happened to him the Viscounts would pay dearly. He began to ride away at a slow trot, then, as he distanced himself from the monastery, began to ease the horse into a gallop until he was deep into the forest. After an hour he dismounted to rest in a shady glade. He was almost asleep when he was alerted by the sound of approaching horses. He quietly rose to his feet, took his sword in his hand and laid his bow and quiver on the ground. He owed a debt to Goles for having remembered to bring his weapons and shield when he had fetched his horse from the stables.

Three knights suddenly rode out of the undergrowth. They stopped and faced William, who glanced around to see if there were other riders. There was a moment's silence before one of the knights took out his sword, raised it and bore down on the solitary warrior.

William stood his ground then crouched and moved sideways, swinging his shield at the rider as he passed, slamming it into his body. Before he toppled to the ground with a thud, the second knight was already bearing down on William with his sword raised. William had just enough time to stab his sword into the fallen knight's body before ducking behind a tree to avoid the second knight's weapon as it slashed downwards, forcing him to ride past without being able to strike a blow.

Without hesitating William knelt down, picked up his bow, slotted an arrow into place and took aim at the knight as he began to turn his horse. The arrow caught him between the shoulder blades and he fell forward over his horse's neck to the ground and was dragged away as the horse bolted, his foot caught in the stirrups. The third rider had seen enough. He turned and rode off at speed.

William stood breathless for several minutes, listening in case there were other knights in the vicinity. There was no sound. He guessed that the knight would return with more troops. Calculating that he had at best an hour's start he mounted and began to ride with all haste towards Falaise.

Night had now fallen and the forest was silent and dark. Towards midnight, sensing danger, William stopped. He could hear the muffled sound of horses approaching. Leaving the path, William eased his mount down an embankment behind a thick cluster of trees. Moments later several horsemen galloped past. Waiting until he could no longer hear anything and the night became silent once more, William urged his horse back towards the path and continued his journey. With the road to Falaise becoming dangerous he had to think of a safer passage. His only chance was to reach Poissy and seek refuge with King Henry of France, his overlord.

It would mean a hazardous journey and a long ride. After what seemed hours, William came to a river and stopped to drink and wash his tired face. As he knelt down he heard a noise coming from behind the trees. He slowly extracted his sword and waited as alert as he could be after the long and tiring ride. He could feel his heart pounding. Someone or something was in the bushes. Whatever it was drew closer until, slowly forcing its way out of the undergrowth, a deer's head appeared. William was not the only traveller needing a drink. Still crouching, he breathed a sigh of relief and smiled as he put his sword away and watched the deer with its nose in the water, quenching its thirst.

"Drink my beauty, drink."

Dawn broke as William reached the coast. He rode along the shore at the water's edge. The only sounds his mind could register, keeping him awake, as the sun began to rise, were the waves lapping on the beach and his horse's hooves splashing in the shallow sea. He was still travelling through the lands of Ranulf de Briquessard, from whom he had just made his escape. William had no desire to make his presence known. He changed his route, riding through the marshes, which led to Ryes. There he knew he could count on the loyalty of Count Hubert, the local Baron.

Hubert had been surprised when the young Duke suddenly rode into his manor unannounced, causing some concern to his guards. But he was made welcome and given a meal by his loyal friend. After a short rest William began to prepare his horse, ready to leave.

"My Lord, stay longer, you need to rest." Hubert advised him. William trusted the ageing Baron. Hubert had always been loyal to his father. But William had other plans. "No, time is short. I must return to Falaise to find Roger," he said, buckling on his belt and straightening the scabbard.

"But the road to Falaise is too dangerous." Hubert was concerned for the Duke's life.

"First Falaise, then France," answered William, his plan already fixed in his mind.

During his flight from Valognes his only thoughts had been to avenge Osbern's death and punish the conspirators for the attempts on his own life. It was apparent to William that he could not fight the rebellious Barons alone. He had already decided to seek the help of his overlord, King Henry I of France. Hubert realised he would not convince William to stay a moment longer.

"As your overlord, King Henry has an obligation to give you his support," he said, "but it is a long journey. I will give you a fresh horse." He beckoned to one of his guards. "I will also provide an escort until you reach Falaise."

After thanking his friend he took his advice and, accompanied by Hubert's knights, followed the winding river through the wooded Orne valley. They had to cross the fiefdoms of Hamon de Dentu, Lord of Creully and Grimoult de Plessis, barons who could no longer be trusted. Nevertheless, fortune was with them. It was an uneventful journey, the only distraction being the occasional boar and birds annoyed at being disturbed while relaxing at the water's edge. On reaching Falaise, William bid farewell to Hubert's soldiers. Roger had been warned by guards of William's arrival with an armed escort and hurried to greet him. Before finding out what had transpired, he invited Hubert's men to rest their horses and ordered servants to prepare some food and wine before they returned to Ryes.

"Where have you been? You look exhausted? What happened?"

"I haven't time to fill you in now. I must go to King Henry at Poissy."

"Henry? What for? Rest first. And you can't go alone," argued Roger.

William was in no mood to listen to anyone. Roger would have no more success in reasoning with William than Hubert at Ryes. William grabbed some meat and gulped down some water before remounting.

"I will return in a few days", shouted William as he dug his boots into the horse's flanks. "Make sure the army is ready for battle. That is all I ask."

Roger could only watch as the dust rose up behind William's horse as it galloped off. He stood for a few moments contemplating what William had said. "The army? Ready for what battle?" Roger shrugged his shoulders. If William wanted the army prepared for conflict, then he must have a reason. He turned and walked slowly back into the castle thinking about how best to carry out the Duke's orders.

CHAPTER 14

William was alone. To reach the French court at Poissy he knew he would still have to traverse fiefdoms controlled by conspirators who would not hesitate to kill him. It was a calculated risk. William kept to the thick forests that covered the Normandy countryside, stopping regularly to listen in case he should meet enemy hunting parties. At one point the woodland ended abruptly. William halted and starred ahead, guessing that the open space ahead was at least three hundred meters wide. Dismounting at the edge of the forest he looked across the field to where the trees began again. The land sloped down into a deep valley where he could make out a river. He knew he was somewhere between Breteuil and Evreux. Keeping to the edge of the forest William guided his horse to the crest of the ridge. From his position he had a perfect view down both sides of the hill into the valleys. Suddenly he picked out what he thought was a reflection caught in the sunlight way below. Straining his tired eyes, William could make out several riders on the bank of the river. They were too far away for them to see him. Keeping out of sight on the far slope William took a deep breath and galloped out of the woodland, not stopping until he reached the protection of the trees on the far side of the ridge.

Several times William had to chance riding across open countryside, but by keeping to the south of the Seine he finally reached France and the safety of the French King's castle at Poissy as dusk was falling. He had spent nearly all day in the saddle. Guards on the wall were alerted when they noticed a horse slowly approach with a prostrate figure clinging to its neck. As it reached the drawbridge one of the guards shouted to the gate master.

"Open up, we have a visitor."

As the drawbridge was lowered the horseman suddenly felt his exhausted body slide slowly off his horse and collapse onto the ground before passing out. The guards hurried towards him, picked him up and carried him into the castle.

The following morning King Henry was holding court with his knights in the great hall of his castle when William made his entrance. He was refreshed and wearing a clean set of clothes.

"Ah, there you are my young Vassal," said the King looking up. "You were in no state to talk yesterday. I thought it better to let you rest. You must be hungry."

King Henry snapped his fingers at a servant. "Bring food and drink for our guest."

William ate ravenously and gulped down wine as he explained to King Henry the events of the previous two days. He listened in astonishment.

"No wonder you were so exhausted after such an adventure."

Finishing his meal, William rose and accompanied Henry to the courtyard where they took a stroll together.

"Hum. So you want my help to rid Normandy of the traitors?"

"I cannot forget those that bore arms against me. I have been planning to remove these rebellious barons for years," answered William in a determined voice.

Henry stopped and turned to him.

"Your father once helped me. As your overlord, I cannot refuse you now."

William clasped Henry's hands and spoke in short bursts.

"I thank you for your support. Roger once said the time will come. It has come. I am now rested enough to return to Falaise. I will be ready within seven days. I will send you notice of where and when."

King Henry nodded his consent and both men turned and slowly walked back towards the main hall each one thinking of how they could benefit from their alliance.

As William rode out of the gates on his way back to Falaise, a solitary figure who had been watching from the ramparts, descended the stone steps and made his way to the main hall where Henry was seated, digesting William's parting message.

"Come Geoffrey, be seated."

"So you intend to give this young bastard your help to unify Normandy."

"He is my vassal."

"For the moment, Henry, but for how long?"

Geoffrey Martel, Duke of Anjou, was resigned to accept King Henry's position whatever his personal feelings were towards the Duke of Normandy. The long border region that Anjou and Maine shared with Normandy was a constant source of conflict, but he was wise enough not to envisage any military confrontation over disputed territory without French collaboration. His ambitions would have to wait.

CHAPTER 15

It was the year of our Lord 1047. Four years had passed since Edward had returned to England where, as was his right and with the support of the Saxons, he had been crowned King. One of his first acts was unworthy of a pious man. He deprived his mother Emma of her estates in revenge, it was said, for having been neglected by her as a child. True to his Norman upbringing, he had surrounded himself with Norman advisors and wished for his close friend, Robert Champart of Jumieges, to be appointed Archbishop of Canterbury.

However, the Saxons did not look favourably on the gradual spread of Norman influence in England. Earl Godwin of Wessex was more influential than ever. An imposing figure with a strong character, he was a man who knew what he wanted. He had been a favourite of King Cnut, who had given him his title in 1018 before his twentieth birthday. He had built up a large landholding and become an influential figure in Saxon England together with his close allies Earl Leofric of Mercia and Earl Siward of Northumbria. Some argued that his wealth and power now came not from his own merits, but through the marriage two years earlier of his daughter Edith to King Edward. A marriage, according to many who frequented the court, arranged by the Earl to favour his own interests.

While Godwin was ambitious, intent on increasing Saxon influence and power throughout England by putting an end to Viking aggression in the north of the country and revolts by the Celts in Wales, Edward's sole purpose seemed to be the construction of an Abbey. He had put his heart and soul into building a house of God at Westminster, by the Thames in London. Consumed by his passion for this monumental project, he had neglected his wife, Edith, who bore him no heirs, and he had momentarily forgotten the growing rise to power of his young kinsman across the sea in Normandy.

CHAPTER 16

While William's mettle was about to be tested in battle, Lanfranc's rise to greatness in the church had been remarkable. Born at Pavia in Italy, he was only about twenty when he had decided to travel to Normandy and pursue his studies at the religious school in Avranches. Devoting himself to the Church, he played a part in extending the influence of Avranches as an intellectual centre far beyond Normandy's borders. In 1040, still in his thirties, he moved on to became a scholar at the Abbey Bec, under Abbott Hellouin, who had built a new monastery. As one of its most illustrious clerics, he ultimately rose to become Prior in 1045. Under his guidance the renown of Bec Hellouin Abbey spread throughout the Christian world. He established a seat of learning attracting many young religious scholars from across Europe. One of his pupils was a young man called Anselmo Baggio. An Italian, like Lanfranc, he was destined to become the future Pope, Alexander II.

Together with Geoffrey, Bishop of Coutances, Lanfranc was acknowledged by the clergy as one of the most able and respected religious teachers in Normandy. His achievements and reputation had not gone unnoticed by the young Duke. William's religious upbringing had instilled in him a conviction and sincere belief in God and the Church and he was acutely aware of the importance of the Papal Curia in Rome. As a means to seek endorsement of his expansionist policies and ecclesiastical reforms, he saw in Lanfranc a useful and wise mediator with the Pope. He also needed reassurance that his illegitimate birth would not be an obstacle in the eyes of the church. Thus Lanfranc, the tall Italian born clergyman, found himself among the Duke's inner circle of loyal and trusted companions in Normandy.

CHAPTER 17

William had made good his promise to Henry. He had taken less than a week to fulfil his mission. With his strategy clear in his mind there was time to see his mother. He had seen little of her over the previous years after she and her husband had moved to Conteville to raise their two children, Odo and Robert. She had always been against violence and disapproved of his warmongering. It had played on his conscience and this could be the last time he saw her. He faced a decisive battle where he would be risking not only his life but also those of his dearest friends. Arlette was pleased to see her son when his arrival was announced. Herluin greeted him then gracefully retired to leave them together. William kissed Arlette on the forehead.

"You look well. Where are Odo and Robert?"

"In the forest. You can see them later."

"Mother I came because there is going to be…"

"Don't. I don't want to hear about your wars."

"It has to be done. Normandy will be unified."

"At what cost? Normans against Normans."

"It is the only way to bring peace."

"Then I can only pray to God for your safety."

William sat in silence turning his medallion over and over between his fingers. He did not have the courage to explain to his mother that the battle he had planned would rage close to her home. He stayed to greet his half brothers, shared a meal with the family, then bid them farewell before returning to his troops.

Eight days after his meeting with the French King, William was ready for battle. It was the 10th August 1047. The previous night, at the head of an army of several thousand men, William had reached Argences, some eight miles east of Caen, where he pitched camp. William had chosen the site as it was mainly flat country, divided by hedgerows and ditches, ideal for Norman horsemen, and close enough to France to enable King Henry and the French army to rally to him quickly.

Meanwhile, the rebel barons led by Guy of Bourgogne had crossed the Orne and only called a halt when they reached the strategic crossroad at Le Croix Caunet. Guy also knew the lie of the land and had hesitated moving his forces closer towards Chicheboville. Before him were wide, flat fields, effective cavalry country. And should the battle turn against him, he could retreat across the river and back to Caen. At 6am on that August day the sun was beginning to rise and William's army was on the move. By 9am they had traversed the Semillon, a stream near Beneauville. The land flattened out as they reached a settlement called Val es Dunes. William could pick out the opposing army in the distance. He spread out his cavalry and brought his archers to the fore.

Under a clear blue sky, the two armies facing each other could see the extent of their opponent's forces and the glint of sunlight on their swords and helmets. Typically, Roger was by William's side. But he could now count on his own friends, Roger de Montgomery, William Fitzosbern and Walter Giffard, young men, now barons, who had grown up with him and stayed close since the years spent together in the monastery. Their loyalty was unquestionable.

Guy of Bourgogne was astride his mount at the head of the rebel barons from lower Normandy who had always opposed Duke Robert's successor. Ever since William had been crowned Duke, Guy had conspired to remove him by fair or foul means. Both Roger and William were in no doubt that he had orchestrated many of the attempts on his life. From the size of Guy's army it was clear that many Normans believed that his cause was just, including some of Robert the Magnificent's own kinsmen. The thread that united men from different parts of the Duchy was that no bastard, born to a peasant girl, was fit to rule the Duchy of Normandy. Riding side by side with Guy were the principal conspirators; the Viscounts of Bessin and Cotentin, Grimoult de Plessis, Hamon de Creully, William Talvas and Raoul Taisson.

Looking at the size of William's army facing them, they were in no doubt that this confrontation would be their last chance. Success on the battlefield meant everything. At stake was nothing less than the Duchy of Normandy. Victory would result in removing the bastard and the control of all the territory between France and Brittany; defeat meant losing all they had stood for and enduring William's vengeance, which would be swift and terrifying. The two adversaries, each with more than one thousand men, stared across the field at their opponents, the heat of the sun starting to make them sweat in their chain mail and helmets. Less than one thousand metres separated the two armies. The rebel forces consisted of foot soldiers, archers and horsemen. The thought must have crossed many a soldier's mind that they would soon be called upon to fight, and kill, fellow Normans, some of whom might even be their own kinsmen.

While Guy was lining up his men and, with the sun slowly rising higher in the sky, William was outlining his plans with his commanders out of enemy sight. He had chosen a hollow protected by a tall hedgerow at the edge of a field. They were standing in a circle holding the reins of their mounts behind them when King Henry arrived. He had left his force of French knights a few hundred metres behind William's lines. The King nodded to the Norman Barons as he joined them and listened to the young Duke.

"Gentlemen, the moment has finally come to end the revolts against me and unite Normandy."

William turned to King Henry and embraced him. "I welcome you. Now that Normandy and France stand together it can be achieved. With your support these Barons facing us today will regret having opposed me for so long."

"I trust that our alliance will deter others with thoughts of turning against you," said King Henry.

"If only it were true, but I think not while Geoffrey of Anjou still has an appetite for adding Normandy to his realm. You know his intentions too well."

The King nodded but did not respond.

William turned to his close friends from the monastery. He placed his hand on William Fitzosbern's arm.

"I welcome you by my side. We fight as one."

William Fitzosbern gestured to his friends.

"We have grown up as brothers. We now stand together as brothers."

"Then join your troops and may God be with us."

William's friends watched the Duke as he led his horse away. Once out of earshot they expressed their feelings.

"I hope he knows what he is doing."

"Do we know what we're doing? I know many of the men facing us."

"Too late to worry about that now."

There were none more loyal to the Duke, but they had long had misgivings about the Duke's motives. They were putting their own lives at stake but there was no change of heart possible now. Whatever their thoughts, they mounted up and joined their troops.

William took up position at the head of his army. His cavalry was deployed in columns across the plain behind three rows of trained archers and five columns of foot soldiers. As had been arranged, King Henry's French army was massed at the rear behind the hedgerows, where the ground fell away slightly, concealed from the opposing forces.

The Rebel Barons' troops had positioned themselves near Croix Caunet, beside the road to Caen. They were spread out in four divisions led by Guy de Bourgogne, William Talvas, Hamon de Creully, and the Viscounts of Cotentin and Bessin. As part of his strategy, Guy had ordered Raoul Taisson to distance his troops to the right to outflank William's army. But his confident expression changed to anger when, instead of staying in reserve as planned, Raoul suddenly ordered his troops to advance halting some one hundred metres from William's lines. Detaching himself from his men he trotted alone towards the Duke who, seeing that he posed no threat, signalled to his line to let him through.

Guy looked at Hamon, his face taught with anger. "Who told Raoul to move forward alone. What does he think he is doing?"

Hamon remained silent, his eyes fixed on William's forces facing him.

Raoul Taisson had never been totally convinced by Guy's arguments, or about fighting the Duke to whom he had once pledged an oath of loyalty. He was a religious man and was not about to invite the wrath of God by reneging on his oath. Riding up to William, he bowed as he said solemnly:

"I gave your father my oath. I gave you my oath. I cannot break my vow. I bid you farewell. May God protect you."

William listened attentively, nodding his head in satisfaction.

"If only others would follow in your path. Go in peace with your men."

Raoul turned his horse to rejoin his knights and both armies could only look on in astonishment as two hundred mounted horsemen galloped across the fields in the direction of Secqueville, away from the battlefield.

"The traitor," exclaimed Guy, angrily. "I will have his body cut to pieces."

"He has left our right flank exposed," retorted Hamon, realising that the loss of two hundred men would be costly.

Guy turned to his conspirators. "Too late now to change tactics. Prepare to do battle and rid ourselves of this bastard."

William calculated that Guy could ill afford to lose some

twenty percent of his troops and decided to strike first in case Raoul changed his mind and returned. He stood up in his stirrups, took hold of his medallion and raised it to his lips. He gave a signal. A trumpet sounded and the archers advanced in unison towards Guy's lines before kneeling and launching a hail of arrows that descended on the first rows of the enemy, bringing down foot soldiers and scattering knights and their horses as they attempted to protect themselves with their shields.

William's soldiers immediately raised their own shields for protection from the expected flurry of arrows, which duly arrived in retaliation. Collecting arrows where they had fallen, William's archers launched another aerial barrage. After several exchanges, which appeared to inflict little damage on either army, William's foot soldiers were ordered to attack.

Guy ordered his own foot soldiers forward. The two armies were now advancing towards each other across the open field, their shouts trying to put fear into their opponents. The armies met in a thunderous clash of steel, as swords, clubs and lances met shields and chain mail armour. Guy then ordered his knights to charge, lances pointing forward. William immediately counter attacked with his cavalry, leading from the front. The galloping horses made the ground tremble beneath them. William charged into the enemy with all his energy, slaying all before him as he attempted to force his way through the mass of bodies and horses to confront the rebel Barons. Norman knights on both sides were engaged in ferocious hand to hand combat. In the heat of battle it was difficult to differentiate between friend and foe as foot soldiers and horsemen clashed. The battle raged beneath a hot sun with neither side appearing to make any progress and casualties mounting.

After hours of conflict William's cavalry began another assault. At a pre-arranged signal, King Henry's French army charged forward from behind the hedgerow across the open country into the enemy's flank. As soon as Guy saw the French appear, he ordered Hamon de Creully's forces to switch direction to confront them. At one point, having attacked from the south, a contingent of French cavalry, led by the King himself, became isolated on a hillock near Saint Laurent. King Henry's horse was brought down in the ensuing skirmish, but protected by his royal guard, he was able to remount and rejoin the battle. The French army was fresher and rapidly began to inflict severe damage on Hamon's men leaving them with heavy casualties. The rebel forces, surprised, outnumbered, tired and outmanoeuvred, were no match for the combined Norman and French armies. They began to retreat in disarray, pursued relentlessly as far as the river at Caen.

William perceived a knight riding away in the direction of La Malcouronne and set off after him. He had recognised Guy de Bourgogne. After a short chase William cornered him in a gully. Dismounting, they faced each other and drew their swords. Guy was no longer a match for the strong and younger Duke of Normandy.

"Guy, I will give you one chance to survive this day. But to do so you will have to run me through."

Guy stared at William, whose face was taut with anger.

"You know that your sword is the strongest in all Normandy," he stammered, tired from the chase.

"It's the only chance you have. Take it!" shouted William as he attacked Guy.

Despite the age difference they fought a long, desperate duel, exchanging blows until Guy was brought to his knees. "I surrender to you."

William was in no mood for mercy.

"I do not want your surrender. Do you not call me bastard to my face like you have done behind my back for so long? You came to fight, so fight!"

William stepped back to allow Guy to pick himself up. Guy placed his hand onto the ground to support himself, but William did not see the handful of earth he had scooped up in the palm of his hand. As he edged closer, Guy threw it into his face, the dust and particles blinding him for a few precious seconds. Believing William to be helpless, Guy raised his sword to strike, but William could just see the blade descending and parried the blow while stepping backwards. Wiping his eyes and angered by Guy's trickery, William attacked him with all his strength. The sound of steel against steel rang out. Guy defended himself well but he was no match for the younger Duke. He finally fell to the ground under the blows raining down, leaving William standing over him, his sword at his throat.

Guy let his sword slip from his hand. "Take me prisoner," he pleaded.

"If you were an honourable adversary I could do so, but I am haunted by a voice from the past that prevents me from exercising compassion."

"A voice from the past? I see revenge in your eyes. But why?" Guy's tone was desperate.

"I could forgive you all the years you conspired against me but a child cannot forget being witness to a foul murder and listening to the screams of a dying man. I have known for years that it was you who had poor Osbern killed. The young servant, who only sought to protect me."

For the first time Guy showed fear in his eyes as he began to recollect the attempt on William's life and the death of Osbern. How could William possibly know, he thought. He was a mere child at the time.

"I... I do not know what you are talking about. I beg you to show mercy."

"The same mercy you showed Osbern? I have lived with this nightmare for almost ten years. I know the real target was me."

Staring at each other in silence with hatred in their eyes, neither Guy nor William had noticed William Fitzosbern ride towards them.

"William, the battle is won. The enemy has fled. We have taken many prisoners..."

He stopped in horror and dismounted as he saw William raising his sword.

"What are you doing? He is your kinsman. You cannot...!"

Guy rose slowly to his feet and stepped backwards as William's sword penetrated his protective chain mail into his flesh. His hand reached out towards William as his legs began to weaken. He could feel and taste blood in his mouth. The last thing he saw was William Fitzosbern's expression of incredulity. Then he felt his body hit the ground before everything went black and silent.

William, casually wiped the blood off his sword, sheathed it and walked past his friend, staring at him as he passed.

"I made a promise many years ago to avenge Osbern's death. It is done."

William Fitzosbern looked at Guy's body then chased after William and grabbed him by the arm.

"I saw hate in your eyes but you cannot rule by the sword."

"Spare me your moral lesson," exclaimed William cynically as he pulled his arm free and strode away.

"And the prisoners. Are you going to put them all to the sword?"

William ignored the question, mounted his horse and rode off.

William Fitzosbern looked up at the sky in desperation. "I ask your forgiveness for him."

Taking a final glance at Guy's prostrate body, he remounted and chased after William. It did not take long for him to catch up as William was trotting slowly back to the battlefield. Side by side, without speaking, they sought out King Henry who was preparing to leave with his army. Henry was looking around the now silent countryside littered with corpses, pretending to ignore the looting of clothes and weapons.

"You have nobody left to fight. Normandy is yours. We can take our leave. But remember, you are still the vassal of the King of France."

William reached out and grasped Henry's hand.

"I shall not forget. Normandy owes you its gratitude. This day could not have been ours without you. I am in your debt. Now I must deal with the prisoners. May God be with you."

William turned his horse and gestured to William Fitzosbern to follow.

As King Henry watched them ride off a French knight slowly approached him.

"Sire, Shall we tend to the wounded and prepare them for the journey home."

"Those that will survive, yes," answered the King. The knight followed Henry's gaze.

"Was it wise to give William your help, Sire? With all Normandy now at his feet your vassal has become extremely powerful."

Henry looked at him thoughtfully. He then turned to watch his vassal riding away until he disappeared from view beyond the trees.

"Perhaps too powerful."

CHAPTER 18

Of the other principal conspirators, Hamon de Creully and Ranulf de Briquessard had been killed in battle and Grimoult de Plessis had escaped, only to be recaptured and taken to Rouen, where he ultimately met his death in suspicious circumstances. Those who had survived were now William's prisoners. Brought to Falaise Castle they were marched into the great hall to stand before the Duke, who was seated on his throne. Gone was their arrogance. They now appeared subdued, dishevelled and tired.

William remembered the voice of the Abbott saying to him "Learn to forgive your enemies." He stood up and started to walk slowly around the prisoners, brandishing his sword and swinging it about.

"For many years you have borne arms against me. I could have you slain now, all of you." He stopped and stared into the eyes of Viscount Neel and William Talvas, which were now expressing fear. "Or leave you languishing for the rest of your lives in dungeons. Maybe have your limbs cut off."

They could not have failed to grasp the message. William moved on continuing to observe the men before him. The tone of his voice became consolatory.

"But I do not want to shed more Norman blood. I do not want to see Normans raise their weapons against each other."

He slowly slid his sword back into its scabbard and returned to his throne. He sat back and gripped the carved lions' heads protruding from the arms.

"You once gave me your oath, do so again. Lay down your arms and swear allegiance to me, William, Duke of all Normandy. I will call a truce. A truce of God, blessed by the Clergy. Go back to your homes and families and live in peace. In return, I give you my oath that under my rule all Normans will be treated fairly in accordance with the law, justice and the church."

The tall slim figure of William Talvas stepped forward. As Lord of Belleme, a distant province, he had already earned the wrath of the Duke for the harsh treatment of his own serfs. He turned towards the other prisoners and then looked at William. The Duke raised his hand for silence.

"My Lord, I speak for all of us. You have seen fit to grant us your pardon and renew your trust in us. We are grateful for your benevolence. In exchange, we extend the hand of friendship and give you our word that we will not bear arms against you again. We pledge ourselves to you and Normandy."

William leant forward, his eyes looking straight at the nervous figure before him.

"Break your word and you will be excommunicated, your estates confiscated and you will be exiled."

All the prisoners nodded their understanding of the consequences and knelt down before William. Their voices resounded around the hall.

"Before God, we do so swear."

The knights stood up, bowed and made their exit. William breathed a sigh of relief. The years of conspiracy and rebellion were finally over.

William Fitzosbern, standing behind William, whispered into his ear.

"Such an honourable decision is the mark of a great leader."

William turned and stared at him with a cynical look. He was going to say something but chose not to. He then turned to Roger, now the elder statesman.

"Remember you once told me I had a mission to go to England. I think I would like to see how Edward rules his kingdom with those Saxon Earls. He pledged loyalty to me. He bears no heir and I am curious to learn who is to succeed him. Now Normandy is at peace it is safe for me to leave."

Roger took William's hand.

"It could be useful. But don't ignore King Henry and Geoffrey Martell. They are now allies and together might pose a threat. I will make contact with Baldwin in Flanders and arrange a meeting when you return."

"I can rely on you in my absence."

"Edward will surely receive you as an honoured guest."

As William made preparations for his journey to England, the dungeon of Le Vaudreuil castle was holding two prisoners, who had been chained for three days without food or water. They were dragged from their cell to a bench where guards strapped them down. They were still asking themselves why soldiers had come to their village at night and had taken them away to the castle when a guard pronounced sentence. The sound of their screams would have left William indifferent as the executioner stepped forward and, raising his axe, sliced off their right hands. Osbern had finally been avenged.

CHAPTER 19

The Saxon Chronicles:
"In the tide of health the youthful monarch offspring of Aethelred ruled well his subjects, the Welsh and the Scots and the Britons also, Angles and Saxons relations of old.

So apprehend the first in rank that to Edward all the noble king were firmly held high seated men.

In this year died Eadsine, Archbishop of Canterbury, and the King gave to Robert the Frenchman, who before had been Bishop of London, the Archbishopric."

After a quiet and uneventful sea voyage, accompanied by trusted barons as a measure of security, William made his way under escort to London where King Edward was in residence, after journeying from his palace at Winchester.

The great hall at Westminster was crowded. William was exchanging pleasantries with Saxon nobles when the sound of trumpets echoed around the room, announcing the entrance of King Edward and Queen Edith. The assembled earls all turned and bowed. It had been ten years since Edward and William had last seen each other. Edward had grown old; his hair and beard had turned white. He made straight for his guest from Normandy.

"Welcome to England, cousin. I trust I have not kept you waiting too long."

William smiled "No, my journey was long and I have been well entertained. I didn't recognize Robert. I was only a child when he left Normandy with you."

He turned and gestured to Robert of Jumieges before acknowledging the Queen. William bowed and gently taking Edith's hand, raised it to his lips.

"I am honoured to be a guest in the house of such a lady. My cousin is indeed fortunate to have taken one so gracious as his Queen."

Edith bowed her head in appreciation. Although now in her mid twenties her appearance was little changed since Edward had first met her; a slight, plain looking woman with short, blond hair. Much younger than Edward, her rise to be Queen had little to do with romance. She had submitted to her father's will and married Edward to perpetuate the Saxon dynasty. The King had not been slow to see the advantages of a union with Godwin's daughter. It would, he thought, give him the full support of the Saxons. That she remained childless had come as a cruel disappointment to Earl Godwin, far more than to Edward.

Edward placed both hands on William's shoulders and they embraced.

"You have grown somewhat."

William looked at him. "You too have become more distinguished in appearance."

Edward laughed.

"It is age and comes from being a King. Come, I hope I can match the hospitality you showed me in Normandy. Tell me how is your mother, and Roger?"

"Growing older, gracefully."

Edward smiled and turned towards the earls.

"You have heard of my cousin from Normandy. I hear he has become a feared swordsman since I last saw him."

"I trust he does not intend to use it against England one day," retorted one of the Saxon earls.

This brought a guffaw from the Saxons, but did not amuse William, as they made their way to the banqueting tables, where a feast had been prepared. Saxon feasts tended to be noisy affairs and, as the guests seated themselves, servants scurried backwards and forwards carrying trays of food and drink, which rarely arrived at their intended table, grabbed by whoever got their first.

Seated next to his guest from Normandy, Edward, who preferred more dignified surroundings, whispered into his ear,

"When you have filled your stomach I have something to show you."

Leaving the earls and guests feasting, Edward, William and Robert of Jumieges took their leave. From the Palace, they made their way across a park on the banks of the river Thames to a vacant plot of land on which were stacked piles of wooden beams and large stones. Edward unrolled plans of a building, which was obviously an abbey or church. It was equally clear that they were standing in the middle of a building site.

Edward showed the plans to William and Robert as they walked around the site. Before Edward could begin to explain his project, William spoke out. He had not come to England merely to look at drawings. There were questions he wanted answered.

"I was surprised not to have seen Earl Godwin or his son Harold at Court. Is it true that they left England?"

Edward looked up from his plans. "They were banished by the Witan."

"The Witan?" enquired William.

"The leading nobles who exercise law in Saxon England. I am merely a King. Godwin and Harold disobeyed my orders to protect Eustace, my brother in law when he was imprisoned by insurgents at Dover Castle. They distanced themselves in France and Flanders but I wager their return to England will not be delayed for long. They have powerful friends."

William could not hide his anxiety about Saxon influence in England.

"Even without knowing him I have a feeling that this Godwin and his family are not to be trusted. I have seen how the Saxons oppose Norman influence. As your kinsmen, we are ready to support you if you need us."

Edward nodded in appreciation. "I thank you for your concern. I know how Godwin schemes. He is an astute political adversary, and ambitious. So is his son, Harold. Godwin may not approve of my Norman advisors here in England, but while I am King I decide who shall be appointed to the court and to the church."

He put his hand on Robert's shoulder.

"My choice of Robert of Jumieges as Archbishop of Canterbury displeased Godwin."

Robert intervened, "I can tell you that when Edward appointed me Archbishop, Godwin's face turned black as storm clouds."

Edward smiled remembering the scene. "I can't say I get on well with Saxons. They are vulgar and ungodly. They don't know what the church is for. Let's just say we tolerate each other."

Edward laughed. "But I would not be King without Godwin and I need Saxon support to keep the Vikings from annexing the Kingdom. The Saxons do not wish to see another Viking on the throne of England."

"Does that include me?" enquired William. "We Normans also have Viking blood."

"If that was the case, Godwin would not have lent me his support to take the throne," responded Edward, becoming slightly vexed by the barrage of questions.

"But your marriage to Edith puts him in a powerful position," argued William. "You have no heir and with so much Saxon support does not Godwin eye the thrown for one of his own sons?"

William paused, mulling over what he had been told about Harold Godwinson.

"I have a feeling our paths will cross one day."

"You speculate too much," said Edward. "Surely you have come here to seek guarantees of friendship not to find my successor. Neither Godwin nor his sons have any legitimate claim or royal blood, but since my mother was your great aunt it is certain that my Norman blood would give you a legitimate claim when the time comes."

William looked thoughtful. Edward looked at him and slapped him on the back.

"Do not concern yourself. I am not yet ready to leave this world."

Edward pointed to the building site.

"Look at my new abbey. I want to build the cloister over there. What do you think? And I will place the altar here in the centre."

They continued to tour the site as Edward enthusiastically outlined his project.

"Your plans remind me of the Abbey of Jumieges," commented William.

Robert instinctively replied. "Where else would he find inspiration."

Their laughter reverberated along the bank of the river. Edward rolled up his drawings and they walked off the construction site to return to the Palace.

It was a cloudy and windy day on the south coast of England as William boarded his longship to return to Normandy. Holding on to a rope as the vessel bobbed up and down in the choppy sea, he turned to Edward who had accompanied him from London with an escort.

"I thank you again for your hospitality. Remember what I said. You can count on my help."

Edward could hardly hear him as the waves crashed around him.

"If I need to call on you, I will do so. But when Godwin returns, as he surely will, he will secure my position and counter any Viking ambitions."

William picked up a thin rolled up packet from the deck and learning over the side handed it to Edward. Reaching out and grabbing it, somewhat puzzled, he unwrapped the gift and saw an arrow.

"A sign of our friendship," said William.

"I will treasure it," replied Edward smiling, remembering the day he had killed the boar in the Normandy forest. "Roger was right."

"About what?"

"He told me your crown would fit you."

"Yours too."

"Perhaps." Edward sighed. "But I wonder if I fit the crown. I am not a warrior but it is a burden we rulers must bear."

"God has given us a destiny, cousin. Yours is to build your abbey."

"And yours?" Edward seemed puzzled.

"Mine?" William pondered for a moment. "Perhaps one day to be crowned in it."

William yelled an order to the sailors and the anchor was hauled up, releasing the vessel into the breakers. His voice drowned by the crashing of waves onto the shore, he called out to Edward:

"I trust the Seigneur will allow me to see your abbey completed. Remember your promise to me as a Norman."

Edward, clearly understanding the significance of his cousin's comments, looked pensive as William waved goodbye. He stayed just long enough to watch William's vessel ride the waves as the sail was raised and its bow pointed southwards in the direction of Normandy.

CHAPTER 20

The sea voyage gave William time to reflect on his meeting with Edward. He had learnt enough to be convinced that Saxon domination in England was a threat to Normandy. He also now had to consider the growing threat from France, Anjou, and to a limited extent, Brittany. King Henry of France was his overlord and had proven his friendship by helping quell the barons' revolts. But William had a suspicion that even after being instrumental in helping him achieve a united Duchy, Henry had plans to add Norman territory to France through an alliance with Geoffrey Martel of Anjou, whose ambitions threatened Normandy's southern territory, and with the Bretons, on Normandy's western border.

Both Roger and William had perceived that it was time to consider alliances to strengthen Normandy's position. Soon after regaining his residence at Falaise William received a reply from the Count of Flanders, his northern neighbour, agreeing to Roger's proposal for a meeting to discuss a closer relationship.

On the day his guests were due to arrive, William was playing chess with his friends in an antechamber of the tower that overlooked the drawbridge when there was a knock at the door and a servant entered.

"Sire there are royal visitors from Flanders."

William turned to his friends.

"Ah, they have arrived. It is time to sit around the table and talk of friendship and alliances."

Leaving the chess table, William wandered over to the window with his three friends. From their position, they could see Count Baldwin V of Flanders, escorted by knights, the Flemish banner flapping in the wind, ride across the drawbridge and into the castle. William took special notice of a carriage carrying three young ladies. From their attire he could see two were maids, but the third had the appearance of someone very special. She was sitting upright, wearing a dark green dress with long wide sleeves with a white trim, her head covered by a white linen wimple, folded under the chin and secured by a headband. It draped over her shoulders and was blowing in the wind. Even with her head covered, her beauty was apparent.

At eighteen, Princess Matilda, the daughter of Count Baldwin and Countess Adela of Flanders was about to meet the Duke of Normandy. She had not particularly relished the idea of travelling to Falaise to meet the young Duke, but her father had insisted and she was old enough to know that alliances between states often meant arranged marriages, like that of her sister, Judith. They had both been brought up in accordance with the strict tradition of the church. Matilda had been taught to read and write as well as master the art of embroidery. She had heard about the Duke of Normandy and his military exploits from her father. But, she thought to herself, if he thinks he can treat me like one of his soldiers, he is mistaken. She was also reluctant to consider a union with someone whose parents had never married. The carriage passed noisily across the drawbridge and through the guarded gate into the castle. Matilda looked up overwhelmed by the magnitude of the walled fortifications and began to feel her heart palpitate. As the carriage approached the castle she would not have been aware of the four pairs of eyes staring down at her from behind the castle walls.

"Is she not a pretty maiden. For what reason has Baldwin brought his daughter with him? Not to negotiate, perhaps to fight?" joked William.

Roger de Montgomery chuckled. "Do you really think she will agree to marry you? She is of undoubted noble origin."

"She does not know what you are like," added William Fitzosbern.

They all laughed.

100

"Come," said William. "Let us not keep our worthy guests waiting."

They descended the stone steps and entered the main hall, already brimming with Norman and Flemish barons. As he opened his arms to greet the Count, William tripped on a step and would have fallen if his friends had not grabbed him. Standing beside her father, Matilda of Flanders put her hand to her mouth to hide her mirth.

William had persuaded his mother and her husband to join them. Count Herluin was a tall unassuming Norman baron with estates in Conteville. After William's father's death, he had accepted him as his mother's husband rather than as a step father. Arlette bore Herluin two sons, Robert and Odo. Although much younger than William, both half brothers remained close and loyal companions throughout his life.

William opened his arms wide and embraced his important guest. The Count had taken the title of Baldwin V in 1036 on the death of his father, Baldwin IV, who was a direct descendant of Elfrida, daughter of Alfred the Great, King of England. The Count was now in his forties with a face, bearing the signs of years of fighting the ongoing war against the Holy Roman Empire, almost hidden by a large moustache and beard. His hair was short and cropped. He wore a cloak, slung across his shoulders, which made him look larger than he actually was. But his presence was undeniable.

"Count Baldwin, we welcome you to our Court."

Baldwin's booming voice echoed around the hall.

"The journey was long but hopefully will be worthwhile."

Baldwin embraced Roger and bowed to Arlette and Herluin.

"What an agreeable surprise that your daughter should bestow her beauty on our castle." said William.

Count Baldwin put his arm around Matilda. She was very pretty but small in stature, much shorter than William. She bowed her head. William bowed to her in turn, took her outstretched hand and gently raised it to his mouth barely touching her skin with his lips.

"You will surely both want to rest and bathe after your journey."

Roger could see the visitors were tired and gestured to servants to guide them to their bedchambers. As they were escorted out, William's eyes were fixed on Matilda. Her smile had captivated him and, when her dark eyes met his, he felt sure something had passed between them.

Later, refreshed and with a change of clothes, the Flemish guests were ushered into the great hall where William offered them places beside him and Roger at the head table. As servants brought food and drink, the invited nobles, who were seated on benches at tables extending the length of the hall, were entertained by musicians and the playful antics of the two inseparable dwarfs and court jesters, Goles and his friend Turold. Dressed in matching costumes, only Turold's beard could tell them apart.

"What an impressive fortress you have," said Baldwin helping himself to chunks of meat. "I would not relish attacking this castle. Fortunately, we come as friends."

William gestured to a servant to fill their goblets with wine.

"I believe it would strengthen our position against France and even England if an alliance be made between Flanders and Normandy," continued Baldwin.

William was not listening, his eyes fixed on Matilda.

"Yes. Sorry, what were you saying. Have another drink."

"A closer relationship between us would make sense."

William was exchanging glances with Matilda who was pretending to look away.

The contrast between them could not have been greater. True to her upbringing, Matilda was eating gracefully tasting small pieces of meat, cut from the flesh and sipping wine from her goblet while William sliced off huge chunks of venison with his knife and stuffed them into his mouth in between slurping down large quantities of wine, using his sleeve like a napkin. Has no one bothered to teach the Duke table manners? She thought to herself.

"I think your daughter would make any man very happy."

Baldwin followed William's eyes to his daughter. He looked exasperated by William's remarks. Wiping his mouth with his hand he spoke with a sharp tone in his voice. "I was thinking of a military alliance between Flanders and Normandy."

Roger was kicking William under the table, not wanting to upset their important guest. William turned to Baldwin, answering him in a more serious manner.

"Er, Yes, of course. I agree with you. Though I fear such a relationship could damage our ties with France."

Baldwin nodded. His wife, Adela, was King Henry's sister. Henry was thus his brother in law and he knew exactly what the French King thought about Normandy.

William continued. "Henry knows that Flanders is strong and a united Normandy has become powerful. There is a risk that he might choose to ally with Geoffrey Martel of Anjou."

"I know Henry seeks ties with Anjou. But England? What about England?

Baldwin was also fully aware that William was King Edwards's kinsman.

"We have a close bond with England so long as Edward is King. But I do not trust those Saxons. It is no secret that they oppose Norman influence. You must know. You gave your consent to the marriage of your daughter Judith to Tostig, Earl Godwin's son."

"A marriage of reason. I didn't want to see Flanders isolated. An alliance makes sense. Let us drink to our friendship." Count Baldwin grabbed his goblet pointing it in William's direction.

"May it be a close one," said William, observing Matilda.

They raised their goblets and drank to a new friendship.

Later that evening, William, having taken leave of the Count and guests, was alone with Matilda in the courtyard. They were walking together along the path below the castle walls.

"So your name is Matilda."

"Yes, and you are William."

From her look she was assessing his appearance.

"You are young to be a Duke."

"I have been Duke since I was eight. It is my destiny to rule the people. I must also keep these ambitious Norman Barons satisfied while constantly protecting Normandy from the warlike intentions of some of our neighbours. I have learnt to deal with such a huge responsibility."

William stopped and bent down, running his hands through roses planted in the garden. He gently snapped a rose from its stalk, placed it carefully in Matilda's hair beneath her wimple and took her arm. Matilda just looked up at him.

"I tell you this because I would ask your father for your hand in marriage. I know I have only just met you, but would you consider such an arduous proposition?"

Matilda was taken by surprise by William's sudden request before they had even had time to converse.

"You are impetuous. I hardly know you yet you wish to take me for your wife. My father has told me about you and I know he would look favourably upon such a union, however arduous it may be. That is why we are here. But I am a princess, you are a bastard."

William's face turned red. He grabbed Matilda by the shoulders and pulled her to him. So close she could hardly breathe.

"Whatever you call me, never call me that again. Never! I will marry you not because of your father but because I want to. Understand?"

William kissed her on the mouth, hard.

Matilda stepped back, her hand on her lips, breathing heavily.

"You are single minded aren't you, and sensitive. I might think about it. But never put your hands on me like that again."

Matilda turned and stormed off leaving William transfixed staring after her. He was not used to such treatment, especially from a woman.

Roger de Montgomery, William Fitzosbern and Walter Giffard were playing chess and were taken by surprise when William suddenly appeared in their chamber. He slammed the door, his face taught with anger. His friends nudged each other.

"It doesn't look too good. What happened?"

"Your charm didn't work?"

William ignored the questions and sat quietly in a corner, his hand on his chin. Sensing his anger his friends sensibly stayed silent.

Baldwin was astonished to see Matilda return so soon. His daughter was plainly annoyed about something.

"What's the matter? What happened?"

"Leave me alone. Can we return home?"

"Already! We came to discuss an alliance."

"Well, you marry the bastard."

"What! You listen Matilda. I am your father. You will carry out my wishes, bastard or no bastard. Is that clear?"

Matilda looked into her father's eyes. "Not now, please. Give me more time."

Not wishing to embarrass or upset his Norman host, Baldwin chose not to ask any questions and, discretion being the best option, made some excuse to Roger and Arlette before taking their leave. The visit concluded without reaching any agreement other than an invitation for William to pursue discussions at a later date.

The Duke of Normandy was not going to allow himself to be rejected. If there was any doubt about his birth, a marriage to the daughter of the Count of Flanders would bring him something he badly needed; respect in the eyes of his followers and God. Moreover, as Roger had pointed out, it was in the interests of the Duchy. After a few weeks reflection he and Roger arranged for another meeting and took a force of Normans to meet Baldwin at Eu castle, a northern stronghold, closer to Flanders.

It had been the home of one of William's guardians when he was a child. Gilbert de Brionne was another loyal kinsman who had been murdered by opponents. By coincidence, after his death, Gilbert's two children had been sent to Baldwin in Flanders for safe custody. As the route passed close to Conteville, William stopped to visit his mother and proposed that Arlette and Herluin accompany him on the premise that their presence might help arrange matters.

Baldwin had spent a frustrating few weeks trying to convince his daughter of the advantages that a marriage with the Duke of Normandy would bring. Despite her reluctance, he persuaded her to meet William again.

Baldwin and Matilda had already taken up residence when William and his contingent arrived.

"Now it is my turn to welcome you," said Baldwin joyfully as he greeted the Normans. "Although I can't call you guests in your own castle."

Acknowledging in turn Arlette and Herluin, he turned and nudged Matilda standing behind him.

"You remember my daughter?"

William exchanged glances with her, slightly bowing his head. Baldwin's eyes followed theirs looking for a sign of reconciliation. There was an embarrassed silence until Baldwin clapped his hands together.

"Well, that's it then. When you've rested we can eat and talk more about our alliance."

As the day was drawing to a close William and Matilda found themselves alone, strolling along the terrace that overlooked the river. Matilda knew she could not refuse her father's wish. Since their first meeting the young Duke had been in her thoughts, and now, alone and close by him, she could sense a growing mutual attraction.

"Well." said William. "Have you thought about it?"

"About what?" answered Matilda, pretending to be ignorant of William's intentions.

William frowned. "About us of course."

"If my father consents, I will be your Duchess." Matilda's voice was casual and distant.

William nodded, trying to appear equally nonchalant.

"That's good. But life will not be easy and there is already one obstacle to overcome."

"My parents will agree."

"No, something else."

"What?"

"The Pope. He will be reluctant to give us his blessing because we have the same bloodline."

"You mean YOUR bloodline."

William's face reddened. He understood exactly what Matilda was thinking.

"I mean OUR bloodline."

Matilda was not sure she understood. "That must be so distant the Pope cannot refuse."

William stopped and took Matilda into his arms. She felt the strength as he gripped her and held her close.

"It doesn't matter. Nothing will stop me from taking you as my wife."

They stood looking into each other's eyes.

Count Baldwin, Roger, Arlette and Herluin, were together in the grand hall engaged in conversation when William and Matilda reappeared.

Baldwin looked relieved.

"Ah, there you are. We were wondering what happened to you both."

"Matilda and I have been talking about alliances."

They looked at each other and held hands.

"Between Normandy and Flanders?" queried Count Baldwin.

"Not exactly. More between Matilda and me. I would ask for your daughter's hand in marriage."

Baldwin scratched his chin. After a moment's silence he spoke.

"Tell me why I would wish for a bastard as my son in law."

There was an eerie silence. Matilda raised her eyes to the roof wondering if the ceiling was about to fall on top of them. Arlette looked at Herluin, stunned. Roger stepped forward as several Norman Barons reached for their swords ready to extract them from their scabbards. William casually wagged his hand up and down to warn them not to react. He turned to Baldwin.

"I will tell you why. Because I will make your daughter a Duchess in the most powerful realm in Christendom and be a staunch and loyal ally."

Baldwin suddenly let out a loud laugh, slapped William on the back and looked at Arlette.

"I meant no offence, nor to you Arlette. I wanted to see William's reaction. He gave me the answer I expected to hear."

Turning to William, he said. "Come let us discuss this, alone."

As William and Baldwin walked around the courtyard deep in conversation, unknown to them, Matilda and Arlette were watching from an upper window. Half an hour later they returned to the main hall. Baldwin looked at William's mother and took his daughter's hand.

"What do you say to this marriage, Arlette?"

"If this marriage pleases you and my son then I am in favour. It is their happiness that is important. Matilda will be like a daughter to me."

Arlette turned to Matilda and embraced her.

"And you Matilda are you sure you want to marry this...Er, Duke?"

"I am father."

Baldwin took his daughter in his arms. He knew she would have to abide by his wishes but it pleased him to know she seemed to have changed her mind and was in favour of the marriage.

"Then so be it. Let us prepare for a wedding."

Turold and Goles jumped around and rolled over in delight while Roger expressed his approval too. "Is there a better way to unite our people?"

While everyone in the room was in high spirits, thinking about a union through marriage, William's mind had reverted to unions of a more military nature. The recent betrothal of Matilda's sister to Tostig meant that Godwin and Baldwin were now linked by family ties forging a Saxon and Flemish alliance. He could understand Baldwin's aim in agreeing to the marriage. It would bring Normandy and Flanders closer together and thus create a kind of three-way pact with England, in which Baldwin would be able to play an influential role. William smiled to himself, admiring the astute mind of his future father in law.

A wedding was thus celebrated in 1051 at Eu castle, the fortress built on a cliff overlooking the small fishing port on Normandy's northern frontier. Preparing for the ceremony, Matilda was in her chamber with maids who were dressing her in her gown. They were joyful and chatting about her clothes and jewellery. Meanwhile, William held office with his kinsmen and nobles waiting for the Abbot to arrive. Looking around anxiously, William whispered in Roger's ear.

"Where is Lanfranc? I must see what delays him."

As Prior of the Abbey of Bec, founded by Bishop Hellouin in 1040, Lanfranc had now earned his place in William's inner circle of trusted nobles. But the marriage of Duke William of Normandy and Princess Matilda of Flanders would have to proceed without papal sanction. He was now in his forties with unfulfilled personal ambitions and defying the Pope was a risk Lanfranc was reluctant to take.

William left the hall to look for him. He found him alone in his chamber pacing up and down with a worried expression on his face.

"Monseigneur, are you ready? It is time to go. Everyone is assembled."

Lanfranc looked at him spreading his arms.

"How can I possibly preside over this arranged marriage while the Pope objects to your union."

"True," said William. "This arranged marriage, as you call it, is to forge an alliance. But it is born out of love. I can tell you our union will endure far longer than Pope Leon."

Lanfranc was pacing up and down.

"I know the blood relationship is distant but there is another matter... your birth. In the eyes of the church..."

William stopped him.

"I am as Christian as anyone else."

Lanfranc was far from convinced.

"Do you realize the risk I would be taking to oppose the Pope?"

"I do, but you are close to him. Marry us, now. Then go to Rome and make your peace. You know you can."

Lanfranc thought for a while as he paced around the room, then sighed.

"You ask a great deal of me. I will bow to your demand. I will go to Rome. But you must understand your wedding will not be consecrated until the Pope agrees. You could even be excommunicated."

William nodded. "Then it is a problem we will have to live with. But I have a proposition for you to take to his Holiness, which should make him change his mind. Can we go now, please?"

William went to the door of the chamber and beckoned to Lanfranc to follow him to the chapel.

The chapel at Eu castle was small. Given the Pope's objection to this union, Lanfranc had wished for the ceremony to be conducted in the most discreet manner. Thus the only people present were Roger, Arlette, Herluin, and Countess Adela of Flanders. Like her daughter, Adela was small and attractive, with blond hair. She was dressed in a long dark blue robe with her head covered by a wimple. When Lanfranc had taken his place Matilda made her entrance, accompanied by her father Count Baldwin. She looked stunning, dressed in a long burgundy coloured gown with gold edges. Her head was covered by a white linen wimple, folded under her chin and held in place by a coloured headband. She wore a silver locket around her neck and two matching bracelets on her wrist. William gestured to Lanfranc to proceed. Lanfranc placed his hand on the Bible and looked up at the chapel ceiling, evidently still worried.

"William, Duke of Normandy, son of Robert the Magnificent and Herleva, ...er Arlette, daughter of Fulbert, wilt thou have this lady as your wife?"

William turned to Matilda. "I will."

"Princess Matilda, daughter of Baldwin and Adela, Count and Countess of Flanders, wilt thou have this man, as your husband?"

Matilda hesitated for a moment looking towards William. "I will."

Lanfranc raised his arms. "The rings, do you have the rings?"

William searched through his clothing and finally found them in a pocket. He gave one to Matilda and they exchanged the wedding rings, sliding them on each other's fingers. Matilda looked at the ring William had given her. It had a gold band encrusted with sapphire.

Lanfranc raised his arms. "In Nomine Patris, I declare you man and wife."

He then raised his eyes up at the ceiling and muttered. "And may his holiness, the Pope, forgive me."

William gave him a despairing look before taking Matilda in his arms and gently kissing her on the lips.

With the ceremony concluded, they made their way to the great hall. As William and Matilda made their entrance the assembled guests applauded. William spotted Turold with Goles and his two young half brothers, Robert and Odo, now in their teens.

"I want you to meet Turold and Goles, our court jesters. Turold is the one with the beard. But do not be fooled by the appearance of Goles. If it wasn't for him I would not be here."

"Then surely he deserves recognition," said Matilda taking the hand of Goles.

"He has received it," said William looking at him and slapping him on the shoulder. "Is that not so?"

Goles nodded in approval.

"And you will have to watch out for my young brothers, Robert and Odo," added William, nudging Matilda and laughing. The two boys started to pull William by the arms in a playful gesture but he pushed them off. William whispered to Matilda as they walked away.

"Odo is already a man of God. He is just fifteen but I have appointed him Bishop of Bayeux."

"Isn't that rather young?" asked Matilda.

William ignored the question as they took their seats. While servants were bringing food and drink, jesters and minstrels took centre stage and the festivities began. Roger de Montgomery turned to William and raised his flagon.

"You have taken a vow of marriage but defied a Pope."

Raising his own goblet, William chose the moment to announce his proposal to the Pope replying in a way that would be clear to everyone present. "Lanfranc is going to Rome to argue my case. I believe the Pope will understand and not look too harshly upon this marriage. I have agreed to build two abbeys in Normandy in his name."

The guests turned to each other exchanging views on the charitable offer to the Pope.

Later with everyone still feasting, William glanced at Matilda and gently nudged her. They rose from their seats and discreetly left the hall, climbing over dogs and musical instruments. Odo and Robert were playing and had not noticed the newly married couple leave. When they turned to talk to their brother, they found themselves staring at empty seats. They looked around in surprise, shrugged their shoulders and returned to their game.

William and Matilda played hide and seek in the castle corridors until they reached the door of a bedchamber. Matilda blocked William as he tried to pass. Sliding up against her, his hand found the handle and, as he turned it, the door opened and they almost fell into the room. William slammed the door behind them and standing with his back to it, slid the bolt, locking them in.

"At last, alone. I was getting bored."

Matilda threw her arms around him. He took her hand and pulled her towards the window where they stood in each others arms looking out across the sea.

"Tell me about Flanders."

"Oh, it is a land of green fields and rivers, not unlike what I have seen in Normandy, full of poppies and tulips."

"You will like it here then."

Matilda gazed up at William. "I will like it anywhere with you."

Matilda noticed the medallion around William's neck and took it in her hand.

"What's this?"

"It belonged to my father. I have worn it ever since he died."

They embraced and their hands started to explore each other's garments. William gently removed Matilda's wimple allowing her blond hair to fall freely onto her shoulders. While Matilda was unbuttoning William's shirt he was finding it difficult to untie the cords fastening Matilda's dress.

"What are you doing?" she muttered impatiently.

"Who on earth dressed you?" William was fiddling with the knots. Finally, the cords loosened and Matilda's dress fell to the floor leaving her in her white underclothes. She dived into the bed and pulled the covers over her. William took off his tunic and let his shirt slip off his shoulders before sliding into the bed where he pressed himself up against Matilda's body.

"You are everything I could wish for."

"Be gentle with me."

"How could I be otherwise, my love, you have such soft skin."

William's hands began to gently stroke her body. Matilda moaned in pleasure as she felt the desire rising inside. They continued to caress each other, their lips and hands exploring every part of their bodies until they were joined in love.

Later, as they lay entwined in each other's arms in the silence of the night, Matilda, her body still tingling with ecstasy, ran her fingers across William's shoulders and down his back. She giggled.

"Your skin is so rough. I can feel your scars. Don't they hurt?"

"Wounds heal", said William, kissing her. "What hurts is the thought that they may not be the last."

They were oblivious to the sound of laughter and music rising up from the main hall below.

PART III

CHAPTER 21

One hundred and fifty miles to the north in another country, in another city, other festivities were taking place. In the great hall of the Palace of Westminster in London, King Edward and Queen Edith, in the company of Saxon Earls, were feasting after a day's hunting. Seated close to the royal table were Earl Godwin and his son Harold, the Queen's brother, and his companion Edith Swanneck. Although Godwin had fathered five sons, Harold, Tostig, Leofwine, Gyrth and Wulfnoth, each of whom had, or would, control substantial land holdings, Earl Harold was Godwin's natural successor.

With a face now weathered from years of hunting in the damp and cold climate of England, his physical appearance made him one of the most feared and powerful of Saxons even though he had not yet reached thirty. Tostig, while possessing the same physical attributes, lacked his brother's strong personality and was perpetually in his shadow.

Nobody seemed to object to the vulgar and loutish behaviour that was common at Saxon feasts. Blond wenches were moving from table to table, carrying trays of goblets filled with ale or wine. They were used to having their bottoms smacked by knights who had been drinking too much, or grabbed for a quick embrace or a kiss. The rowdy mob was burping and swearing as overflowing goblets of wine and beer were being slurped down, their contents spilling over clothes. Chunks of meat were sliced off venison and pork with daggers and stuffed into open mouths. A few revellers, too drunk to care, were climbing onto tables only to fall off to the delight of everyone present. Morgar, a knight, rose from his seat waving his goblet, hardly able to stand.

"I raise my... I raise my gobl... I drink to King Edward and Earl Godwin who gave us this shline...fine feast after a day's hunt."

Earl Harold, who was also under the influence of drink, shouted at Morgar.

"You have drunk enough ale for all of us today."

The sound of laughter echoed around the hall, and when Morgar, teetering on the edge of the table, finally lost his balance and collapsed onto the laps of several knights, his weight overturning the bench seat, taking all with him onto the floor, there was even more merriment.

Amidst all the revelry King Edward looked bored. His ecclesiastical upbringing in Normandy had inspired in him a sense of dignity and respect. His facial expression had not escaped Earl Godwin as the small group of Edward's Norman friends including Robert of Jumieges, played chess. Godwin, helping himself to a chunk of meat and laughing, nudged his close allies and powerful land owners, Leofric, Earl of Mercia and Siward, Earl of Northumbria, who with their blond hair, moustache and beard could have been brothers. "Look at them my friends. They do not know how to amuse themselves. Let us raise our flagons to Saxon domination of England."

Leofric whispered into his ear. "Do not air your thoughts aloud. Edward relies on his Norman friends."

"Ah, Edward is getting old. Let him build his Abbey, we will decide England's future."

Seated at the same table, the Saxon Bishop Stigand watched and listened without joining in the conversation. Godwin glanced towards the King and slapped his son, Harold, on the back.

"Tell your sister to wake up the King. We have much good meat to eat after the hunt."

Harold looked at Edith and murmured in her ear. "Is not the King hungry?"

Edith gestured to Edward who declined more food or drink. Tostig, becoming somewhat irritated at the way the King was being teased, turned towards his father.

"Let the King be, father, he is tired after such a long day."

"Ah, Tostig you are forever taking sides with the King," mumbled Godwin, filling his goblet.

"Better Tostig than the Normans," interjected Harold to laughter from the Saxons. Tostig did not appear amused at his brother's remark. Neither did Edward's Norman friends.

King Edward suddenly rose to his feet and the guests all looked up.

"No, please, continue with your feast. I have other matters to attend to."

Leaving Robert to ponder over the chess board he walked out slowly, leaving the earls to pursue their feast. Godwin, seeing him depart tapped Harold on the shoulder and they both rose and followed Edward. They found the King in his chamber as usual studying the plans for his Abbey.

"Sire you are spending too much time on this building and not enough on affairs of state." Clearly inebriated, Godwin had difficulty standing up straight.

Edward did not look up and continued to study his plans.

"Look Godwin, look at this. Do you not think that affairs of state are trivial compared to this magnificent Abbey for the Lord. It will stand as a glorious monument to our achievements long after we have departed from this earth."

He finally looked up. "What affairs of state do you have in mind?"

Godwin leaned over towards Edward, burped and spoke seriously.

"We must protect the country from the Vikings and Celts whose ambitions to divide the kingdom never cease. Can you not see that the longer we wait, the greater the risk to your crown?"

Edward continued to study his plans.

"Your concern is reassuring, but I sense that it might have more to do with expanding your estates. Is it not so?"

Harold, who had been listening in silence until then, intervened.

"Sire, the country can never be united so long as Harold Hardrada of Norway claims the throne."

"I know it. And what of our Norman cousins? William also has plans to succeed me. Was it a coincidence that you both returned to England so soon after his visit? You never accepted Robert de Jumieges as Archbishop and contest the appointment of Normans to every influential post."

Godwin glanced at Harold somewhat surprised at the King blurting out his grievances.

"We only seek what is good for England, Sire."

"Yes, I am sure that is so," said Edward, not bothering to look up.

"You must give your assent to deal with the revolt in Wales."

"Are not Harold and Tostig capable of handling the revolt with sufficient men at arms?" asked the King.

Harold turned to his father and with his encouragement answered the King.

"We can count on Leofric in Mercia, Sire. Together, we will crush any resistance."

Edward, still looking at his plans, sighed.

"Then take the army west in my name. But I hope when this matter is done you will finally accept Robert as Archbishop. Now if that is all, I would like to get back to my project."

Godwin and Harold looked at each other and took their leave.

Edward had no illusions about Godwin ever accepting Robert as Archbishop. His one ambition was for Saxons to rule the country. When the Witan had declared Godwin undesirable, Edward knew he would not remain out of the country for long. Less than twelve months after their forced exile in Flanders, Earl Godwin had returned to England with his sons. They had become increasingly frustrated by the King's appointment of Normans to positions of influence. Making certain that he could count on the support of the leading Saxon nobles and the loyalty of Saxon soldiers, Earl Godwin reached London by sailing up the river Thames with an army. Edward had neither the capacity nor the inclination to engage in a civil war and capitulated. Thus, Godwin renewed his authority and influence as undisputed leader of the Saxons.

He had built himself a substantial manor several miles from London. His landholdings were extensive, covering thousands of acres, and the peasants and fyrds who lived in the many villages on his estates, toiling his land in order to make a meagre existence, were always complaining about the taxes they were forced to hand over. They also knew that when Godwin needed troops to defend his land, or his country, they could not refuse taking up arms.

Two hours after leaving the King in London, Godwin, Harold, Tostig and Stigand were riding through the village and up the tree lined path that led to the manor. They entered the courtyard, where servants were waiting to take care of the horses and lead them off to the stables. Harold enjoyed his hunting and was arguably more concerned about his hounds and falcons than his family. Edith Swanneck, Harold's companion, had arrived earlier but before giving her so much as a glance, Harold greeted his hounds, which were running around him, their tails wagging, happy to see their master return. He then watched two falcons circle overhead before swooping down to land at his feet. He picked them up one by one and after stroking the two birds of prey handed them to a servant who put them back into their cage. Then he turned to Edith and kissed her. Following Danish tradition he had not married the blond, pretty girl of nineteen, but out of their union came five children. He embraced the eldest who had come running from the house, teasing him before handing him to his mother.

Having washed and changed their clothes, the family gathered around the table to eat. After the meal it was customary for the ladies and servants to retire, leaving the men to talk alone.

Godwin paced around the wood panelled chamber summing up the situation.

"The King is preoccupied with his monument to posterity. So best leave him to it while we look after our own interests. We have the King's authority to put down all attempts by Celts or Vikings to usurp any part of ..."

Godwin stopped in mid sentence at the sound of the door creaking open.

Someone was listening. Harold went to the door and pulled it open.

"I have caught a spy," he exclaimed, chuckling as he took one of his sons in his arms. He called for a nanny, who came and quickly took the young child away to bed. The room became quiet as Godwin continued.

"...to usurp any part of this Island. Once we control Wales we must look to rid the country of the Vikings and these Normans who bore me with their intellect and preaching. You are both aware that Edward is getting older and Edith will not provide him with an heir to the throne."

He put his hand on Harold's shoulder.

"You will succeed him."

Harold nodded without expressing either surprise or gratitude at his father's remark.

In contrast Tostig's face went white. He could not hide his feelings. He knew that the childless King had always looked favourably upon him, ever since he had been a young boy, but Harold had always been closer to his father. Godwin stooped to put a log on the fire. As he did so he lost balance holding the wall to stop him from falling.

"Father, are you all right?" Tostig moved quickly and held out his arm.

"It's nothing. It is nothing," Godwin replied, breathing heavily. He turned to look at Stigand.

The short, fat, balding Bishop of Winchester whose round, flabby face was usually a deep shade of pink, had been a long, standing advisor to the King. Edward disliked him intensely but he had to compromise in order to satisfy the Witan. Now, at sixty, Stigand was about to become the most powerful clergyman in England.

"Stigand, you have served your country well. You will be appointed Archbishop of Canterbury." He paused. "After we persuade the King to remove Robert of Jumieges."

Stigand was nothing if not pompous, as well as greedy, but his religious upbringing had made him a cautious man.

"I would be honoured to accept such a position but the King will not remove Robert voluntarily. Even if you obtain the support of the Witan, the Pope must give his approval."

In Saxon England the Witan could not be ignored. As the governing body of the state, formed by sixty senior Saxon nobles and clergymen, its approval was required for all senior appointments and religious decrees. Harold voiced his fears.

"It would be dangerous to go against Edward's Norman friends before he officially appoints an heir."

Godwin was clearly irritated by his son's remark. He had no intention of allowing King Edward to choose his successor.

"I have submitted to the King's demands to leave Hakon and Wulfnoth, our kinsmen, hostage in Normandy as a gesture of my good faith. You and Tostig can deal with the Welsh situation. I will discuss the matter of succession with the Queen."

Godwin looked at Harold. "If anyone can influence Edward it is your sister. Now let me rest."

CHAPTER 22

The road to Rome was long and tortuous. Lanfranc first made his way to the Benedictine monastery at Cluny in central France. Founded in 910 AD, the monastery, covering nearly two acres, was one of the most important religious centres in the Christian world. After spending a few days in the confines of the Abbey he continued his journey, crossing the Alps and sojourning in the town of his birth, Pavia, where he met old acquaintances he had not seen for many years. The last stage of his journey took him through Florence and Orvieto before finally reaching Rome. As a child in Pavia, Lanfranc had always dreamt of visiting Rome. Now he was returning again. Reaching the city his route took him past the Coliseum, now falling into disrepair, and through Constantine's gate, to the Forum, where he paused to admire the ruins of the Roman Empire. He had read some of the teachings of Emperor Marcus Aurelius and admired his philosophical guidance. Lanfranc walked along the banks of the Tiber until he reached Hadrian's Mausoleum. Then, following the covered colonnade built for pilgrims, he passed through the gated entrance in the fortified walls of the Basilica of St Peter at the foot of the Vatican Hills. He was escorted to a wing of the Basilica, which had been built as the Pope's residence. Supported by massive circular columns, the vaulted central nave rose to a dome in the centre through which rays of light shone down onto the marble tiled floor.

His arrival was announced to Pope Leon IX, who had agreed to receive him that same afternoon. Waiting in the Pope's chapel, Lanfranc paced up and down rather than spend the time in prayer. He had been too concerned about his audience with the Pope to admire the architecture of the Papal Curia. His thoughts turned to the spiritual reflections of Marcus Aurelius:

"Whatever happens to you it is for the good of the world. That would be enough right there. But if you look closely you'll

generally notice something else as well: whatever happens to a single person is for the good of others."

The sound of a door opening brought Lanfranc back from his thoughts to his imminent appointment with the Pope. He looked up to see a priest beckoning him to enter. He was ushered through a corridor into the Pope's private chamber. The chamber was in stark contrast to the hall. It had white walls and the vaulted ceiling had been formed from wood panels. A single opening at high level provided natural light. At one end of the chamber Pope Leon IX, flanked by two robed cardinals, was seated on an ornamental throne on a raised platform. Born near Colmar in 1002 to a deeply religious and noble family, his path to Rome had also been long and controversial. Twenty years as Canon at Toul had prepared him for the Pontificat. He stared at the tall figure making his way towards him.

"Lanfranc. It is a pleasure to welcome you to Rome," greeted the Pope.

Reaching the base of the platform, Lanfranc knelt and kissed the Pope's outstretched hand.

"You Eminence is too kind. I express my gratitude for allowing me this audience at such short notice."

Pope Leon learnt forward.

"I am always interested to hear about the church's progress in far off regions. Perhaps you are ready to explain the purpose of your visit. It must be of some importance for you to make such a long journey."

"I am here, your Eminence, at the behest of Duke William of Normandy."

"Ah yes, I thought so."

The Pope raised his finger at Lanfranc. "You realise that by presiding over this marriage, you acted against papal interdiction. I could have you excommunicated."

"The Duke is a very persuasive man your Eminence. I only acceded to his demands on the basis of a promise which he asked me to convey to you."

"And what exactly does he think he can offer that would require me to counteract the laws of the church forbidding such marriages."

"I know that your eminence has reason to fear..."

The Pope cut him short.

"I fear no one but God."

Lanfranc thought for a moment.

"... to be concerned about the ties between Normandy and Flanders which this union has cemented. But the Duke wishes to assure you that their alliance harbours no designs on the German Empire upon which you rely."

"Do I?" interrupted the Pope raising his eyebrows.

Lanfranc continued.

"By the powers vested in him and as a mark of his faith, the Duke has raised money to build monasteries, nominate bishops and bring about church reform throughout Normandy after the destruction caused by the Vikings."

Lanfranc paused.

"Go on," said the Pope.

"He now sees a similar threat looming from Saxon domination in England. King Edward was forced by Earl Godwin and his Saxon allies to remove Robert of Jumieges and instate the Saxon priest, Stigand, as Archbishop of Canterbury."

"Hah." The Pope slapped the arm of his chair. "Stigand is corrupt and will never receive the Pallium from me. He prefers to fill his fat belly and his pockets, not the church."

The Pope sat back in silence then spoke.

"How could Duke William be in a position to bring changes to the church in England?"

"King Edward has no heir, Eminence," continued Lanfranc. "As his kinsman William has a claim to the throne. Papal support could only strengthen his claim. As King he would most surely back the reforms you seek."

"Hum. I see," said the Pope learning back. "But his birth poses a problem for the Church."

"Your Eminence. Can it be just to punish a child for his parents' lapse of faith."

The Pope considered Lanfranc's plea for a moment.

"But you still have not told me about this promise."

"Should your eminence choose to give your blessing to the marriage, ignoring the question of birth and the very remote blood relationship, the Duke will build two abbeys in Normandy in your name, in Caen."

The Pope sat back scratching his chin.

"In Caen? Very well, but I will need to think this over. I will convene the cardinals. You will have an answer in due course. Now I have other matters to attend to. You know you are always welcome. I bid you a safe return."

Lanfranc bowed and stepped back.

"Your Eminence," he said, before being escorted out of the chamber.

Once outside, Lanfranc stopped and looked up. With the warm Rome air caressing his cheeks he smiled to himself, pleased with the outcome of his meeting. Marcus Aurelius had indeed given him wisdom.

When Lanfranc next visited Rome, Leon IX would no longer be Pope.

CHAPTER 23

Saxon Chronicles:
"In this year died Godwin the earl on the seventeenth before the kalends of May."

A few weeks after taking the army to Wales at the King's command, Harold and Tostig returned from their expedition to their manor. They had carried out their father's wish and with the help of Leofric, the Saxons had quashed the Celtic rebel uprising. From the window of their first floor chamber, Queen Edith and Edith Swanneck saw the two riders approaching. Looking distraught, they hurriedly left the chamber, and descended the stairs to greet them. Having handed their mounts to servants, Harold and Tostig pushed open the front door, chatting as they made their way into the hall.

"Home at last. We can tell Father that we put them to the sword and taught them a lesson they won't forget."

"I have reason to think he will appreciate more the land we now control."

Harold embraced Edith Swanneck who was looking anxious. Harold noticed that Queen Edith had tears in her eyes.

"What is it?"

"I have been waiting for your return. Father is sick. You must hurry."

Harold and Tostig looked at each other in shock.

They hurried upstairs and entered Godwin's chamber. Godwin was lying in his bed, his head propped up by a pillow, surrounded by his close friends and family. A priest was present. They parted to allow Harold and Tostig to approach their father. They knelt by his bed.

"Father, with Earl Leofric we now control all the country west of Mercia. They won't rise up again," said Harold, hoping to convey some cheerful news.

Godwin was weak but he found the strength to talk.

"That is indeed good news. We are so close to establishing a Saxon nation. But it is too late for me. I will not live to see it."

He waved a hand towards Stigand, who, not wishing to disrupt the priest's prayers, kept at a discreet distance.

"I told you Stigand would become Archbishop of Canterbury. It is done."

Harold and Tostig both seemed stunned by the revelation.

"With the full backing of the Witan," Godwin added, as if to justify his decision.

He grasped Harold's hand.

"It is up to you now. You need to be closer than ever to Edith and Tostig. You know the King has always trusted him. I have provided for Gyrth and Leofwine. You will succeed me as Earl of Wessex but I always wanted you to become King. Don't worry about Edward's Norman friends. It is within your grasp. Take it."

It was obvious from the look that Tostig gave Harold that his envy had not diminished. Harold, still kneeling, glanced at Stigand, put his mouth close to his father's ear and spoke slowly but persuasively.

"You have made us the most powerful family in the land. Who can stop me now?"

Godwin was weakening. He looked at Edith and took her hand.

"My daughter, Queen of England."

Edith bowed down to kiss her father's forehead as Godwin gave a sigh and closed his eyes, his hands dropping by his side. The priest began to administer the last rights as they all quietly left the chamber.

Outside in the hall Harold stood by the window, staring blankly across the fields. Edith Swanneck sidled up behind him and placed her hands on his shoulders.

"Let me comfort you in your grief. I know how close you were to your father."

Harold put his hand on hers. "Thank you. Thank you."

It was the 14th April 1053.

PART IV

CHAPTER 24

Over the next decade, the Saxon hierarchy underwent a transformation as the older generation passed on. While Harold took over his father's estates in the south, his brother Tostig was rewarded by King Edward, who appointed him Earl of Northumbria, succeeding Siward who had died in 1055 with no heirs. In 1062 Harold's close allies, Edwin and Morcar, became Earls of Mercia. Godwin's ally, Earl Leofric, had died in 1057 but his son, Alfgar, only survived him until 1062, thus leaving the Earldom to the two grandsons, who remained loyal to Harold.

Under their leadership the Saxon clan continued to increase their land holdings, extending their influence and power across England, and as such were able to contain the threat posed by Viking aggression. The King, still engaged in the building of his monumental Abbey, had granted Harold powers of state, which strengthened his position as the most influential Saxon in the land and as the brother to the Queen, a potential successor to the throne.

At the same time the church was also going through a period of change, bringing with it intrigue and conflict. Robert of Jumieges, removed as Archbishop by Godwin in 1052, had been forced to return to Normandy. Pope Leon died in 1058 before, to William's regret, ever granting papal approval to his marriage to Matilda. Without authority from Rome, Stigand's influence on the Church as Archbishop of Canterbury remained limited until the new Pope, Benedict, granted him the Pallium. However Benedict, in a move that shook the very foundations of the Church, was declared uncanonical. He was removed in 1059 in favour of the Bishop of Florence, appointed as Pope Nicolas II.

Lanfranc managed to persuade Nicolas to accept the marriage but he only remained in office for two years before being succeeded in turn by another Italian, Anselmo Baggio, the same young disciple who had studied under Lanfranc at the priory of Bec Hellouin. He took the title of Pope Alexander II. It was thanks to this relationship, that Alexander II, as head of the Catholic Church between 1061 and 1073, would give papal support to William in his quest to take the crown of England.

CHAPTER 25

In the Duchy of Normandy, although still resentful of his English cousin for having allowed Godwin to remove Robert of Jumieges as Archbishop of Canterbury, William was preoccupied with the military ambitions of Anjou and France. After Val es Dunes William had remained on good terms with King Henry, his overlord. In 1052 while hunting together they had received news that Geoffrey Martel had stormed the fortress at Alencon and occupied Domfront on the border with the duchy of Anjou.

"Alencon is a strategic border site," Henry told William, "It would be a threat if you allowed it to stay in Geoffrey's hands."

William needed little encouragement.

"I will recover Alencon."

Having brought peace to Normandy, William knew he could count not only on the support of all the barons in the Duchy but also the people of Normandy; the peasants to whom he had become a hero. He immediately set in motion his plan to push the over-ambitious Geoffrey Martel back to Anjou. Moving south from Falaise, at the head of a powerful Norman force, William recaptured the town after a short skirmish. Geoffrey had left a small troop in charge of the garrison with little chance of defending his prize. News of the success of the expedition spread far and wide. Not because of the speed of William's victory, but because of the cruel revenge he inflicted on Alencon's inhabitants. Before attacking the stronghold they had dared to scream abuse at William from the ramparts, calling him all manner of names and reminding him of the nature of his birth. This so incensed William that he showed no pity and cut off the limbs of several of his luckless prisoners.

Not all his commanders agreed with the Duke's reaction. William Fitzosbern had already seen that William's temper was short and that he could explode whenever mention was made of his illegitimacy. However, nobody could dispute William's brilliance as a military commander. Having recovered Alencon with so little opposition, taking advantage of his army's presence on the border with Anjou, William advanced along the valley to repossess Domfront castle, which was no less strategic than Alencon. After a siege, which lasted through the winter of 1052, the castle finally fell with hardly any loss of life. Geoffrey Martel was left with little choice but to order his remaining forces to return to Maine.

William was still engaged at Domfront when a messenger arrived with reports that a kinsman, William of Arques, in the north of the Duchy, had rebelled against him with the backing of King Henry's French forces and declared himself Duke of Normandy.

"Have I been deceived by my own overlord?" William gasped to his commanders in disbelief. "Our army could not be more distant. We cannot remain here while the Duchy is under threat."

It did not take William long to fathom that Geoffrey Martel and King Henry had joined forces. A trap had been laid. While William's army would be tied up along the southern borders, Henry imagined he could advance unopposed from the East to join his kinsman at Arques. It was a carefully prepared plan aimed at annexing the Norman Vexin to establish a unified French province. But it did not allow for William's creative mind or his military acumen. Neither Geoffrey Martel nor King Henry could have envisaged the loss of Alencon and Domfront so effortlessly, or the speed with which William could move his forces.

Within three days the Duke had crossed Normandy with his army and began another siege, this time surrounding the town of Arques on the northern border. He had marched his troops more than two hundred kilometres. The occupants refused to surrender, but William was patient. His forces outnumbered the French. He would starve them out. It took several weeks before the garrison finally capitulated. After Alencon, William Fitzosbern was expecting the worse from the Duke, but to his surprise and relief, William chose to be lenient and spared both his kinsman and his men at arms.

William then set about protecting the long southern border. As a clear demonstration of the superiority of the ducal army, William invaded Anjou and built a castle at Ambrieres. His brother, Robert, was put in charge of the castle at Mortain, like Domfront on the road to Brittany, while to protect the Duchy from France, William built a castle at Breteuil, near Evreux, which was assigned to his loyal companion, William Fitzosbern. The Duke was thus able to complete the annexation of the whole of the southern border region to his realm and consolidate his power.

This episode reinforced William's fears about his overlord, the French King. Incensed at the friendship that William had established with Flanders through marriage and, obsessed at the increasing dominance of Normandy, Henry was now more determined than ever to crush the power of his Norman vassal. The decision he took would ultimately lead to his downfall.

Geoffrey Martel II Duke of Anjou, known as the hammer, had succeeded his father Fulk III in 1040 when he was thirty four years old. He had little reason to like the young Duke of Normandy, whose growing military power always posed a threat. When King Henry offered him the hand of friendship and sought to form an alliance, Geoffrey Martel needed little encouragement. He remembered their previous alliance during the winter of 1042 and 1043, when they had successfully laid siege to Tours. They had joined together again in 1051 to win control of the city of Le Mans. The loss of his northern garrisons had been a final humiliation after ten years of military campaigns on Normandy's southern borders. The bastard, upstart from Normandy would be no match for a united French and Angevin army. Geoffrey Martel was at Le Mans when his guards announced the arrival of the French King.

As the dawn mist swirled around the castle moat, Geoffrey climbed to the ramparts to see the King of France with a small mounted escort clatter across the drawbridge. Descending to the great hall, he welcomed his guest and ordered food and drink to be served.

"We are clearly of the same mind," said Geoffrey after listening to King Henry's account of the siege at Arques. "The ambitions of the Duke of Normandy must be curtailed before we lose all our strongholds and perhaps even our kingdoms."

Henry looked concerned. "Our plan failed and William will now be on guard. We will not be able to fool him again."

Geoffrey nodded, realising that their chances of removing the Duke of Normandy were diminishing as he grew stronger.

"The next time may well be the last opportunity we have. We cannot afford to make any more mistakes. Our allies in Brittany will rally to our side."

"I fear they are too distant to join us. Anyway our combined army will finally crush him," said Henry, menacingly, his hand gripping his goblet so tightly, his knuckles turned white. King Henry and Geoffrey Martel spent the next twenty-four hours walking, eating, drinking and planning. By the time the French King left Le Mans to return to Poissy, they both knew exactly what had to be done.

It would be the most powerful military offensive William would have to deal with in Normandy. By 1054 King Henry and Geoffrey Martel had formulated plans for a major attack on the Duchy. King Henry crossed the Seine near Evreux with Geoffrey Martel's forces while the French army, led by the King's brother Eude, was advancing further north aiming to squeeze William in a vast pincer movement. William had no choice but to defend Normandy against this dual threat.

Ten years of conflict had transformed the Norman army into an efficient and well tried fighting machine. The French would soon learn to their cost that few could match the disciplined Norman cavalry or the combined force of archers and foot soldiers in action. From the safety of his castle at Falaise, William had sent out scouts who were keeping him advised of his enemy's movements. For the first time he had given his brother Robert his own command, bestowing upon him the title of Count of Mortain.

When reports reached William that the enemy was on the march, he outlined his plans to the Norman Barons whom he had summoned and who were now grouped around the table in the castle hall. Nobody questioned the ability of William as a military strategist. They listened carefully as he told them of his intention to divide the army into two forces to counter the threat. Robert would take one army with Count Eu in the north across the Seine to prevent the enemy advancing on Rouen. William would lead the second force in the south towards Evreux to block off Henry and Geoffrey Martel's army before they converged in the east. There was no feasting that night. Before any extended expedition, William preferred to retire early and expected his commanders to do likewise. He needed to be fully alert to confront what was a critical situation for the future of the Duchy.

The next morning the Norman forces were lined up in columns in the valley below Falaise castle. Matilda could only watch apprehensively as her husband prepared to depart for yet another military conflict. William embraced Robert and William Fitzosbern and wished them good fortune as they moved off northwards with one division before he joined Roger de Montgomery with the other army and set off in an easterly direction.

By the time Robert's army had crossed the Seine, the French forces had already reached the small, fortified town of Mortemer, north east of Rouen, without opposition. Having marched across open country with no sight of the Normans, they were confident and had set up camp. However, they had not counted on the effectiveness of Norman intelligence. Scouts were relaying reports passed to them by peasants in every village. Robert's army encircled the French camp and at dawn the Norman cavalry backed by infantry took the French, still sleeping, by surprise, inflicting a severe defeat. When King Henry learnt that his army had been annihilated by Robert and that he would still have to face William with the other division, he retreated back to his own lands. Nevertheless, despite the French losses at Mortemer, it failed to deter Henry who would confront his Norman vassal again in what would be a decisive confrontation.

King Edward asking Harold to visit William in Normandy

23.

AMENTVM:FECIT: HICHAROL:D:DVX:
LMO DVCI:-

KING EDWARD ON HIS DEATHBED

29. 30. 31.

E·IES·
hIC·DEDERVNT:HAROLDO·
CORO NA· REGIS
hIC RE SIDET:HAROLD
REX·AN GLORVM·
STIGANT
ARChI EPS

36.

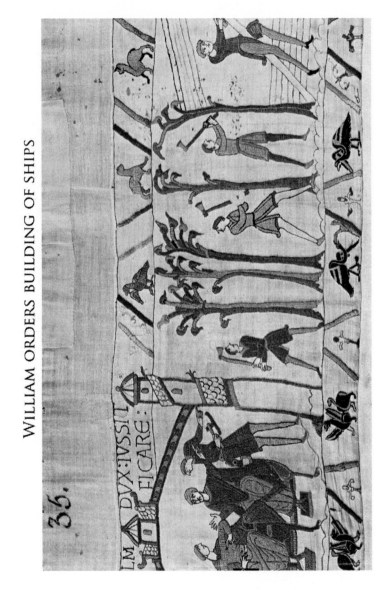

SAXONS & NORMANS IN BATTLE

A NORMAN ARROW PIERCES HAROLDS EYE

CHAPTER 26

Three more years passed. In April 1057, having failed to learn their lesson, Henry and Geoffrey Martel had not given up on the Norman Duchy. They had rebuilt their armies and led a combined force across the Seine towards Caen destroying villages and pillaging as they swept across the Vexin. Revenge had perhaps clouded their judgement. The Duke had presumed, quite reasonably, that after Mortemer both King Henry and Geoffrey Martel would have given up their attempts to remove him. But it was not so. The latest incursion persuaded William that he had to inflict such a crushing defeat on his French and Angevin neighbours that it would end the wars between them. Always an astute strategist and knowing the lie of the land, William had anticipated that the French and Anjou forces would follow the roman road to Rouen. It passed through the village of Varaville where they would have to traverse the river Divette, a few kilometres inland from Dives where the river flowed into the sea.

William knew the terrain well. Across the wide estuary the terrain was marshy with an intricate network of streams. He could count on another ally; the sea. At high tide it swept inland submerging the marshes, forming a vast shallow lake. The thick woodlands close to the river provided William with excellent cover and, unknown to either Henry or Geoffrey, he had concealed both his infantry and cavalry so that they had a perfect view of the Divette at a bend where there stood a wooden bridge. This was one of the few crossing points. The French would have to cross the river somewhere.

When William's scouts returned with news that they had sighted the enemy, William waited patiently, his army watching the enemy troops slowly marching towards the bridge. When they reached the banks of the river, William ordered his knights to advance, deliberately making their presence known. Feigning an orderly retreat, they encouraged the enemy forces to pursue them across the river and over the weak, timber bridge into the marshes. As William had predicted the bridge would not support the weight of horses and armour. The timbers gave way and the bridge collapsed. Henry's army was left floundering as the rising tide seeped across the estuary into the marshes leaving them stranded. They were totally at the mercy of William's archers, foot soldiers and peasants who had joined the fray. French and Angevin soldiers were up to their knees in rising water, struggling to free themselves, weighed down by chain mail. They were sitting targets for Norman archers who could choose their victims at will, dispatching repeated flurries of arrows into their bodies. Mounted knights, unseated from their horses, drowned under their weight. Those that succeeded in reaching the banks were cut down by foot soldiers and any that managed to reach the forest, faced the swords and lances of Norman cavalry.

King Henry and Geoffrey Martel could only watch in horror as their army was decimated. It was a costly reverse. The pain of defeat was too much to bear and they returned to their lands demoralised and weakened. William's success removed forever the threat to Normandy from France and Anjou. It also served as a warning to William's opponents in Brittany, who would realize that they were no match for the Norman forces and would be wise to avoid provoking confrontation. Success on the battlefield was followed by another stroke of good fortune for William. In 1060 both King Henry and Geoffrey Martel died. Henry would be succeeded by his son Philippe, but he was only seven years old and posed no threat to Normandy.

While he was growing up, Philippe's mother Anne of Kiev was appointed Regent, a position she shared with another leading noble. His name was Count Baldwin of Flanders.

CHAPTER 27

William was now the uncontested master of the Duchy. To complete the annexation of the border with Maine, in 1063 the Duke's army successfully captured the southern fortresses of Sille le Guillaume, Beaumont sur Sarthe and Mayenne. He had a staunch ally in neighbouring Flanders, and, through succession, his traditional enemies in Brittany, Anjou, Blois and France were now weak.

Nevertheless, William had decided to erect a new castle on a strategic site at Caen. It was a virtual citadel. It stood on a hillside close to the banks of a river only a few kilometres from the sea, a formidable stronghold covering several acres protected by thick outer ramparts. Inside the grounds a chapel, stables and lodging quarters had been built. To the north of the site, a deep moat encircled ramparts with four circular towers at each corner. To gain access meant crossing the drawbridge and passing below the single main gate tower leading to the courtyard in which there stood a virtually impenetrable square keep. The keep had thick stone walls rising twenty metres high. It was here that William had arranged his residence with kitchens, living quarters, storage rooms and a well to supply water.

He could, perhaps for the first time in his life, forget about wars and conflict, concentrate on managing the affairs of Normandy and spend time with his family, bringing up his children. William had changed. His hair was still short and cropped around his head but the moustache had gone and, while the eyes were the same blue, his face was tougher and his expression hardened by the years of war. Despite William's absence fighting wars and protecting the Duchy from aggression, he had spent enough time with Matilda for her to have given birth to three boys and two girls. Robert, the eldest was twelve Richard eight, William three, Cecily two and Agathe one.

Looking down from the window in amusement at the antics of their young nephews and nieces in the courtyard, Robert and Odo, William's half brothers, had grown into mature young men, members of William's inner circle of loyal companions. Robert had earned his respect at Mortemer, while Bishop Odo had become one of Normandy's principal ecclesiastical dignitaries. They watched as the servants brought the children inside to rejoin their parents. Robert tried to attract William's attention as one of his children toddled over to his brother.

"Well, was it the right decision to move the court here to Caen?"

"This stronghold is both larger and easier to defend. The river Orne gives us better access to the sea and we are nearer our Flemish allies."

Acknowledging William's reasoning, Robert changed the subject.

"Do you realise two years have passed since the deaths of Henry and Geoffrey Martel?"

"And ten years since our mother died, God rest her soul. I have earned these last five years of peace after Varaville and now Henry and Geoffrey are both dead France and Anjou will never rise against us again."

"But with Normandy at peace you seem to have forgotten the worsening situation in England. King Edward is getting older and Saxon influence is spreading."

Odo was quick to intervene.

"Since Godwin died, Edward has bestowed powers upon Harold. He exercises control over affairs of state. With no direct heir to the throne, he is in an influential position to take the crown."

William was listening at the same time as watching his young son.

"Robert, stop that!"

Seeing his son kicking his baby sister, he smacked him. Robert ran to his mother crying.

"You hurt him," complained Matilda.

"He must learn to take punishment," said William unmoved.

"Why?" answered Matilda. "So he can grow up like you."

William gave her a hostile look and turned to his half brothers.

"Where is the problem? So long as Edward is King there is nothing I can do. He gave me his word, did he not?"

"But the Saxons have always sought to remove Norman influence and place their own people in every post," said Odo.

"I have known that since I went to England."

"Then how can you accept Stigand as Archbishop of Canterbury? It was Godwin who removed Robert of Jumieges. Without the Pope's approval and the Pallium, Stigand cannot preside legitimately."

William tried to calm Odo.

"You react as a man of the church. But I cannot interfere while Edward is King. Do not forget that Norway too has a King who eyes the throne of England. That Norseman Hardrada is a foe to be reckoned with and he does have a claim. The Saxons know that."

William was silent for a while. Then he continued.

"Thanks to Edward we hold two of Harold's kinsmen hostage in Normandy. This is not something he will tolerate indefinitely. Harold will surely seek to bargain for their release. He will come."

William paused for a moment. "England made me welcome. When Harold comes I will make him welcome. Then we shall see who will be King."

Odo and Robert turned to gaze out of the window as William forgot about England and continued to play with his children.

CHAPTER 28

King Edward was sitting in his chamber at Westminster Palace as usual, huddled over the plans of the Abbey being built on the banks of the Thames. He looked up when he heard the door opening. A servant was standing at the entrance. "Earl Harold, Sire."

"Out of my way." Earl Harold brushed past the servant, nodding for him to close the door behind him. "Ah, there you are," said Edward, his voice becoming softer. Harold could not fail to notice that the King's health was deteriorating and he was looking frailer.

"You have been asking for me."

"I require a service of you. I am getting too old to make long journeys."

"A journey? Where?"

"I want you to go to Normandy and discuss my succession with Duke William, my cousin."

Harold frowned, taken aback by King Edward's suggestion.

"Your succession? With that Norman?"

"I want to see Normans and Saxons living side by side after I'm gone. No more conflict."

"What about my kinsmen, Hakon and Wulfnoth still being held there? I have been expecting you to negotiate their release. You still bear favour but I fear some Normans may not take kindly to a Saxon visitor."

King Edward looked at Harold.

"Well, you have not exactly endeared yourself to them, have you? I arranged with your father to send them to William as a guarantee of your father's loyalty. Regrettably, he did not keep his promise. But they should not be punished for your father's failings. I will prepare a letter for you. It may be fortuitous for you to deal with this personally and meet William. I know that my cousin will treat you well. Now let me rest."

Edward put his arm on Harold's shoulder and escorted him to the door. Alone again, the King gazed out of the window towards the Thames, mindful of his age and what he was asking. As he watched the waters flowing eastward towards the sea he sighed.

"To think the future of England depends on the intentions of the Duke of Normandy."

Before leaving for Normandy, Harold went to his sister's chamber to inform Queen Edith of his conversation with the King. He had asked Tostig to join them. As Tostig sat silently by the window watching the Queen busy with her embroidery, Harold paced up and down pondering over the King's request.

"The King wishes that I meet Duke William in Normandy... to discuss his succession."

Tostig was taken by surprise.

"You think he has William in mind to succeed him?"

"I do not know the King's mind, but I shall not give up one single field of Saxon land."

"What about Hakon and Wulfnoth?"

"I intend to obtain their release."

"The Duke must have been delighted to learn that Stigand is Archbishop," said Edith sarcastically. "Especially without the Pope's blessing."

Edith constantly had to endure Edward reminding her of Godwin's dislike of his Norman friends.

"Edith," said Harold firmly. "I know you are close to Edward, but he is busy with his abbey. I have no intention of allowing either the Pope or William to intervene in our affairs. The King wishes that I meet his cousin. I will see how powerful a Duke this William is and whether he has ambitions in England. I will decide what action to take on my return."

Harold was already regretting having left England. He had not chosen the best of times to make the voyage. Although it had been cloudy before embarking at Bosham, the weather had worsened during the crossing. He wondered whether praying for a safe voyage at Bosham Abbey before the journey had been a good idea. The rain was pounding his vessel and the rising north easterly wind was churning the waves. The small boat was being buffeted around in the raging waters like a cork, becoming increasingly difficult to control. Even with the sails lowered, the sailors struggled to keep the vessel afloat. Once the French cliffs had been sighted they hugged the coast heading south towards Normandy, hopelessly attempting to resist the wind and current that kept pushing the vessel closer to the shore.

"The wind is too strong my Lord. I fear this strong current will force us to beach before our destination."

Harold was holding onto the mast as the small vessel lurched from side to side, turning his insides upside down. Trying not to fall, he shouted back to a sailor.

"The coast is near. Try to find a protected bay where we can land before we are thrown onto the rocks. Don't damage our vessel."

Harold grabbed an oar and helped the sailors strain to guide the vessel, which was being pounded by the waves as it was pushed inexorably towards the shore. Miraculously avoiding the submerged rocks that dotted the bay, the vessel finally beached with a grinding sound throwing its occupants to the deck. As the sailors endeavoured to cope with controlling their vessel, Harold stepped off onto Norman soil. The rain suddenly ceased. Wiping the water off his clothing, he looked around perceiving that they were in a small, rocky cove surrounded on three sides by cliffs.

Unknown to the Saxons, who were busy securing the boat, they were being watched from the cliff top by soldiers who had seen the vessel approaching. They waited until the ship had beached, assessing the number of its occupants, before riding down the narrow path to the shore. Harold was unloading the horses with the sailors, when they found themselves surrounded.

"Who dares set foot in Normandy with such stealth."

Harold looked up at the cold eyes staring at him from behind the conical helmet. He was wet and dirty after the crossing, and tired. He counted the soldiers facing him and, wise enough to realise that he and his men were outnumbered, saw no point in resisting. But he was not going to cower before anyone.

"I am Earl Harold of Wessex, son of Godwin. We were forced ashore by the storm. I am here to talk terms with Duke William about my kinsman. To whom do you bear allegiance?"

"Count Guy de Ponthieu from Hesdin. We will take you to him." responded one of the soldiers casually, seemingly unimpressed.

They began to lead the Saxons away unaware that a sailor was still on board the vessel. He had heard the soldiers approaching and flattened himself down on the deck, pulling a tarpaulin over him. He waited until there was silence before daring to peek over the gunnels. When he was certain he was alone, he jumped down to the beach, climbed the path and started to run along the cliff top in the opposite direction to that taken by the soldiers.

It was dark as the guards at Caen Castle made out three Norman knights approaching. They were accompanied by a tired, bedraggled looking man. One of the knights called out.

"Lower the drawbridge, we bring news for the Duke."

Duke William was holding court. He was seated in the main hall with Roger, his brothers and friends when the sailor was brought in. He had a worried expression on his face as he stood before the Duke.

"Sire, we found this man wandering near the shore," said one of the knights. "He claims to have landed with Earl Harold of Wessex."

William looked around at his companions, then at the sailor.

"Earl Harold? In Normandy? I told you he would come. Where did you say you landed?"

The sailor began to mumble.

"I cannot say for sure, Sire, a small bay to the north. I managed to hide in the vessel. I heard soldiers mention a Count Guy de Ponti or something. Then they led them away."

William let out a loud laugh and slapped his knee.

"Count Guy! Then we know where your Earl is."

He gestured to a knight.

"Give this man food and shelter. Send soldiers to Hesdin with a dispatch I will give you for the Count ordering him to release the Earl and his sailors immediately. Then bring them here to Caen. Oh, and send the Count my greetings."

Robert looked at William inquisitively. "And if Count Guy refuses?"

William sat back and gave his brother a cynical smile. "Refuse! He will not refuse. He knows what would happen."

The following morning the sun rose early with a chilling north east wind blowing as Earl Harold, escorted by Count Guy's soldiers, rode along a deserted beach scattering the seagulls that were scavenging for food. The sailors and personal escort of housecarls who had accompanied him from England, followed behind, grouped together in a horse drawn wagon. They came to a halt when they found themselves facing eight mounted knights lined up less than one hundred metres away. After a moment's silence, two of Guy's knights beckoned to Harold to follow and they began to ride slowly towards the group facing them.

When they had reached mid way the two knights, without any word of warning, wheeled round, and rejoined the other knights guarding the wagon. Ignoring the Saxons, The Count of Ponthieu's escort turned and galloped off disappearing over the dunes in a cloud of sand. Harold, facing the horsemen alone, remained motionless in his saddle, his long hair blowing in the wind, watching and waiting. He became slightly anxious as one of the knights started to ease his mount forward in a slow trot. Harold's eyes never left him as he came nearer, riding up to his side.

The knight's eyes peered out from behind his helmet. He released the reins and slowly removed his helmet. Harold saw a slightly tanned man with virile features and cropped hair smiling at him. Then a hand stretched out.

"Harold?

"William?" exclaimed Harold, still not certain of the identity of the man facing him.

"Welcome to Normandy," said William. "So we finally meet face to face."

The two men clasped hands and looked into each other's eyes. If either of them were casting their minds ahead or had any reason to believe that this meeting would result in conflict over a crown, they did not show it.

"I wanted to greet you personally. I hear you had a miraculous landing."

"No miracle, just good seamanship and a bit of luck."

"God sometimes assists," said William not expecting to convince Harold.

"I trust Count Guy treated you in the manner to which an English Earl is accustomed."

"My landing and brief sojourn with Count Guy was neither planned nor enjoyable," responded Harold curtly. "I thank you for your intervention. I have heard much about you from your cousin. He sends his greetings."

William nodded his gratitude then spun his horse around.

"Come," he said. "And tell your men to join us."

Harold waved to the bedraggled crew in the wagon and began to follow William. As Caen castle came into view, Harold's eyes widened, visibly stunned by the immensity of the walled, Norman stronghold. Once safely inside, they dismounted and their mounts were led away to the stables. William escorted Harold to the great hall to be greeted by

Matilda, his children and several Barons. Harold approached Matilda and gently kissed her hand.

"I am honoured to meet you. Your grace and beauty remind me of your sister, Judith. It makes me think that perhaps I too should seek a wife from Flanders."

"Thank you. I think that would be a good choice," responded Matilda, smiling.

Harold looked at the children. "I see you have a line of heirs."

William smiled, patting one of his sons on the head. "At least my succession is assured. But they have a long time to wait. I am not ready to give up the Duchy. Come, you must be hungry after your journey. We can discuss the purpose of your visit at the table."

Matilda interjected. "I am sure Harold would like to bathe and rest before eating."

"Of course," said William, apologetically.

"That would be most appreciated. I trust my men will be looked after."

Matilda beckoned to a servant to take Harold and the sailors to their chambers.

"I will see they are well taken care of."

An hour later Earl Harold, refreshed with a set of clean clothes, joined his hosts. In the vast banqueting hall, he was given a place of honour next to William and Roger. Matilda sat with her ladies in waiting. William's eldest daughter Edwige, still a child, was staring at the blond haired stranger from England. As food and drink were served, William engaged Harold in conversation. Matilda watched shaking her head at the table manners of the two men cramming food into their mouths and slurping down wine.

"How is my cousin? He must have built his Abbey by now."

"Not yet. After all these years it's still unfinished. Edward is becoming frail and I don't know if he will survive long enough to see his work completed."

William and Roger glanced at each other furtively.

"You are here to discuss the matter of your kinsmen, is that not so?"

"You are well informed."

William served Harold then filled his own goblet.

"I have to be in order to survive. There are still some who would like to see the back of me. I will arrange for you to meet your kinsmen. But while you are here you will have an opportunity to see how Normandy is ruled and partake in some hunting. Don't you think so, Roger?"

Roger raised his goblet in approval. "An excellent idea. I will attend to the preparations."

Harold bent down and retrieved a small packet. "Edward gave me this for you."

William opened it. He removed a long thin shaft and held it between his fingers.

Harold frowned as he saw what the packet contained. "An arrow?

"It is a private matter between us," answered William, chuckling to himself.

CHAPTER 29

The evening tide was rising. Six armed riders were galloping along a path through the marshy fields that led to the sea, as if pursued by some unseen enemy. Before them, rising up out of the waters stood a dark, forbidding, stone fortress. Conceived as a Benedictine monastery some hundred years before, the Abbey of Mont Saint-Michel had become the most important religious sanctuary in the Duchy. It was constructed on an island, with the only access to the mainland submerged during high hide. Built on granite rocks, the construction of the Abbey had been a daunting enterprise, taking its toll of lives. The massive steep, stone, walls rose to a height of more than eighty metres above sea level. Over three hundred steps had to be climbed to reach the abbey. The lower crypts led to three levels of galleries, linked by a series of corridors and stairwells. At each level, stone pillars supported the floor above.

Mont Saint-Michel was more than just a sanctuary; it was a stronghold on the Breton border. By the time the knights reached the causeway the sea was beginning to wash over the rocks onto the track, swirling around the horses' hooves. When they reached the gates, one rider hurriedly dismounted and hammered his fist on the heavy wooden gate. The young man, looking more mature than his twenty-six years, knew that he would be able to rely on the hospitality of the Benedictine monks. After a few minutes there was a sound from within and a panel in the door slid open to reveal a pair of eyes peering through.

"Open up, we seek refuge," implored Conan of Brittany.

"This house is open to all who seek sanctuary within its walls," replied the voice softly from behind the door. A few minutes later the heavy gates creaked open and the horsemen rode swiftly into the sanctuary. Once the riders were safely inside, the monk gave a cursory glance at the rising waters swirling around the walls and pushed the gates firmly shut behind them.

CHAPTER 30

As a keen hunter on his estates in England, Harold relished the opportunity of joining the Duke and his entourage in the forests of Normandy. Hunting was in his blood. He had risen early to prepare the falcons William had offered him. As Roger and William stepped out into the courtyard they were surprised to see him dressed and, with the falcons on one arm, playing with the hounds. Servants had already saddled the horses and prepared the wagon with provisions. Harold stroked the falcons before gently handing them over to a servant and took the reins of the horse William had chosen for him. After having made sure that everyone was ready, William shouted to the guards for the drawbridge to be lowered.

Leaving the castle and Caen behind them, the hunting party followed the river Orne through dense green woodland. After an hour's ride William called a halt and they dismounted to eat and drink. Wild boar and fowl were plentiful in the forests and together William and Harold made several kills before returning to the castle later in the day with a heavily laden wagon. They entered the drawbridge side by side.

"From what you have shown me of Normandy I can understand your attachment to this land," said Harold admiringly.

"I love this country. As you, I am sure, love yours." replied William, pleased to have shown his English guest the Normandy countryside where he had spent his life.

As they were dismounting a messenger approached. "My Lord, we have learnt that Count Conan has led a raid on Norman soil. He has sought refuge in the Abbey at Mont Saint-Michel."

"When? Where? Are there any victims?" William fired away with questions. "Did he cause any damage?"

"I do not know, my Lord. It was a few days ago."

William looked at Harold and slapped him on the back.

You see what I told you. Not everyone agrees with my policies."

"Who is Conan?" enquired Harold.

"One of my neighbours who thinks Norman territory belongs to him. Brittany is not sufficient. You have a chance to join an expedition to find out the purpose of his incursion. We have had a good day's hunting. Tomorrow will be another good day. Only this time it will be a manhunt. Let's rest. It's a long journey and we leave early in the morning."

Despite the early morning chill Matilda had risen with the children, covering them to keep them warm. They watched from the ramparts as William, with Harold and a troop of Norman cavalry, rode out of the castle. She knew their journey would be long but had grown accustomed to William being away, sometimes for long periods at a time. After more than twenty years being married to the Duke, she had also learnt to give up worrying about whether her husband would return from his military campaigns. She had her children to bring up and played a significant role in managing the affairs of the Duchy. William rarely had time to handle day to day administrative functions and had learnt to appreciate his wife's role. She watched until the riders had disappeared from view into the rising mist before hurriedly taking the children indoors out of the cold.

Riding side by side through the countryside William was taking every opportunity to get to know his English guest.

"I spent such a short time and saw so little of England. It must be far larger than Normandy?"

"From north to south it can take a week's march," replied Harold. "I should know I have travelled it. It takes longer to cross my own estates than today's journey."

William pointed to the countryside.

"God has blessed Normandy with such fertile land."

"I can see. But you saw the green fields of England. All the land between London and the south coast now belongs to me," said Harold, asserting his own status.

"Really," said William pretending to be impressed.

Suddenly it began to rain. Harold and William both looked up at the sky before covering their heads.

Harold smiled. "And the heavens often open up and drown us with water too."

They both laughed.

"Take refuge at Cerisy Abbey." shouted William to his troops, beckoning them to follow him.

Fifteen minutes later the tower of Cerisy Abbey could be seen rising above the trees. The Abbey had been built on the banks of a lake and was reflected in the water, potted with ripples as the rain continued to fall. Circumventing the lake, the troops reached the Abbey entrance. After dismounting and tethering their horses they shook the rain from their clothes and sought shelter beneath the porch. William pushed open the heavy doors and they filed in, their footsteps making a resounding echo on the stone floor.

Leaving the knights to dry themselves, William showed Harold around the sanctuary.

"My father built this Abbey as a haven of peace to seek solitude from the wars. He specifically chose this site for its remoteness."

William paused and glanced down at the floor. "Unfortunately, he didn't derive much benefit from it. It was completed just one year before he left for Jerusalem."

William's thoughts went back to the last time he had seen his father. Despite the passage of time he could remember this pious, bearded man, dressed in a pilgrim's cloak lifting him up and sitting him on his knees to explain the purpose of a long journey he was about to make.

Harold was observing the massive stone walls and columns as they made their way along the aisle. The vaulted roof had several slit windows to give the effect of space and light. But with grey clouds covering the sky the interior was dark and sombre and torches had to be lit. William took Harold around the cloister and through a small door to the refectory to join the knights for a meal. After they had rested and eaten William cleared a table with a swipe of his hand and laid out a map.

"Let us finalise our plans to deal with Conan."

The knights all gathered round.

"With Mont Saint-Michel built on an island I have an idea to flush him out."

William explained what he had in mind.

Fifteen minutes later, after nodding their understanding, the knights retired to their dormitory leaving William alone with Harold. Taking with them a cask of wine and two goblets, they made their way to a small chamber where a fire had been lit. They sat down near the chimney. Harold filled his goblet.

"In all my travels in England I have never seen such castles as I have witnessed in Normandy.

"Perhaps you have less enemies," suggested William. "Our castles have always had to withstand the warlike ambitions of our neighbours in France, Maine and Brittany. Ever since my childhood, this has been my way of living. I have moved from one castle to another surrounded by horses, soldiers and Barons who want my blood."

Harold sympathised with his companion but wanted to make a point.

"England is also plagued by rivalry. You saw that for yourself. But any resistance to Saxon rule is met with force and quashed. Nobody is going to take my country from me."

William understood the rather blunt message.

"I will challenge you."

"Challenge me?" Harold looked startled.

William pointed to a chess set laid out near the fireplace.

"You do play?"

"Of course."

Neither could claim to be masters of the game, recently introduced into Europe after originating in Asia. But it would not have been right for either to imply any weakness. The two men pulled up chairs and sat down facing each other close to the fireplace. As they poured drinks, William threw a log onto the smouldering fire. Shadows flickered across their faces.

William gestured to Harold. "As my guest you have the first move."

They sat in thoughtful silence for a while concentrating on the chess board with its small carved stone figures. Harold advanced the pawn in front of his bishop two spaces. William considered the move, noticing it would give Harold the chance to use his bishop, and countered with one of his pawns, leaving an opening in front of his queen. He looked up at Harold.

"You have not taken a wife. But do not tell me that in your youth you did not chase and seek pleasure with all those blond English wenches."

Harold immediately advanced another pawn. It was Harold's turn to look thoughtful and respond.

"Of course I did. Like all young men. Her name is Edith. She has given me children. But we never took vows because neither she nor any of the other English maidens in my company were good enough for my father. He was always looking for someone fit to be a future Queen of England."

William had noticed Harold concentrating on advancing his pawns one by one. He moved a knight into a space in front of his pawns.

"You do not use your knights? Pausing for a second, William added. "Really, so you do have ambitions to be King?"

"It was my father's wish," said Harold, considering William's move. "I prefer to establish a defensive wall."

It was obvious to Harold that William was trying to prove his superiority.

"Knights do have the advantage of being mobile. They can penetrate a defence," retorted William. "And now is it your wish to become King?"

Both men knew that the game of chess was not going to be just a way of passing a pleasant evening in front of the fire. They filled their goblets with wine as they continued to play.

"There are many contenders," said Harold, not wishing to give a direct answer while he reflected on William's strategy.

"There is always a risk of knights being exposed to a second line of defence."

William pursued his quest for answers that had little to do with the game of chess.

"Like Hardrada for example? And what about my own claim?"

Losing his concentration William made a tactical mistake exposing one of his bishops to Harold's pawns, which Harold removed with glee.

"That was en error William, I have your bishop."

William looked annoyed. The wine was beginning to have an effect as the two men played what was becoming a danger-ous double game.

"A Norman bishop taken by a Saxon. That rings true."

William moved his queen diagonally across the board towards Harold's King, which he had to protect with his castle. It was Harold's turn to frown but it was also his move and he chose a direct approach.

"You want to claim Edward's crown?"

William took the bait.

"I believe the king is vulnerable."

Harold tried to dissuade his opponent.

"For the moment he is well protected by the queen, soldiers and castle."

Harold paused, then sensing William's intentions, continued.

"With Normandy to rule, surely you would not wish to engage in conflict with Vikings and Saxons in a large, unknown country across a hostile sea?"

William helped himself to a chunk of meat. Without looking at Harold, he answered quietly and with a hint of cynicism. "The sea never deterred the Vikings."

Harold nodded thoughtfully and moved a pawn closer to William's king.

"Hum", said William. "You are edging closer to the king. Without support is that wise?"

"Better to take advantage of every opportunity."

"But is it within your power?"

"That depends on your next move."

William slid his queen closer to Harold's rook.

"I may have to attack your castle."

Harold, sensing danger, chose to counter attack by moving his queen into an attacking position. Realising what Harold had in mind William said:

"You still have to take the king."

Harold was now concentrating on defeating William.

"Is that not the object of this game?" I have you in check."

William realised that Harold's move had put his king at risk. He sat momentarily in silence looking at the board.

Then he made an astute manoeuvre. An opening allowed him to place his remaining bishop where he could protect his king and simultaneously threaten Harold's queen.

"Ha! Now you are vulnerable to my bishop."

"Harold pondered for a moment, assessing the possibilities. "Hum, I think it wise to stay this contest on equal terms."

William, now clearly tired from too much wine, sat back and looked at Harold.

"Perhaps you are right. There will be another time. We have to rise early."

Harold finished his drink, stood up and staggered to the door, unintentionally pulling it open so hard it slammed into the wall. As he shut it behind him he heard a voice, the words penetrating through the door. "Only one of us will be King."

William sat staring at the fire, reflecting on whether anything had really been achieved by the evening's conversation, until in an act of frustration he raised his arm and wiped all the pieces off the board and across the floor. Then he sat back, put his leg over the arm of the chair and raised the goblet of wine to his lips. Looking down, he retrieved a piece near his foot. It was Harold's king. "Only one of us will be King." he repeated quietly to himself, squeezing it tightly.

CHAPTER 31

Dawn was breaking as William, Harold and three knights reached the coast. They dismounted and tethered their horses to trees. Moving slowly towards the shore, staying hidden behind tall reeds, they looked across the bay. Only the spire of Mont Saint-Michel was visible through the sea mist, which shrouded the abbey. William's small group was making its way slowly along the water's edge when they found a small craft anchored in the shallow, murky waters. William signalled to the two knights to bring it in closer. As they started to wade out they felt their bodies beginning to sink very slowly into the sand under the weight of their chain mail.

They dared not shout for fear of announcing their presence. As quietly as possible, they called out to William.

"Sire. Sire, I am sinking. Help."

"Me too, the armour is weighing me down. Do something."

William turned to the other knight.

"By the devil!" he gasped. "Quicksand! Quick, bring the horses and some rope."

The knight hurried off to fetch a horse. When it was close to the water's edge he unravelled a rope tying one end to the pommel of the saddle and throwing the line to the knights wallowing in the sands. As they reached out it fell short splashing into the water. Harold, who had been a spectator, quickly stripped off his own protective chain mail, took the rope and began to wade out towards the two knights, whose knees were by now submerged. "Here, grab the rope. We will try and pull you clear." As Harold advanced he could feel his own feet beginning to sink into the soft sand.

William stood and watched anxiously as Harold waded in as close as possible holding the rope. He threw it forward and this time it was grabbed in panic. Once one of the knights had secured it around his waist Harold gestured to the other knight holding the reins of the horse.

"Now pull, slowly."

"Be as quiet as possible." whispered William.

The knight enticed the horse backwards tugging on the reins, and one by one the frightened knights were gradually pulled free from the quicksand. Back on solid ground they lay down, relieved, and began to wipe the mud from their legs.

"Thank God for that," said Harold, calmly wiping the mud off his boots.

"Are we converting you?

Harold grinned as William slapped him on the shoulder.

"Thank you for your quick reaction," continued William. "It was a brave act. We could all have perished."

The danger over, William could not afford to waste more time.

"Forget what has happened. It is clear that we cannot cross from here. Try and find another boat further along the shore."

They stalked cautiously along the bank, through the mist, treading carefully through the reeds until, by chance, they found what they were looking for. The small boat had been pulled up onto the shore and whoever had last used it had left the oars secured inside. Grateful for their good fortune and making sure the horses were tethered and concealed, they boarded the tiny vessel, untied it and pushed it out into the bay. Fortunately, the mist had not dissipated. The sea and sky merged into a gray mass. They rowed slowly, with only the sound of the oars dipping into the water breaking the silence. They could barely make out the silhouetted Abbey before them. William touched Harold's shoulder and whispered to him.

"I hope we are not too late. Otherwise my plan will fail."

As he spoke the sound of horns could be heard from the other side of the Abbey. He looked relieved. Following the Duke's orders, after allowing what they thought had been enough time for him to reach the rear of the Abbey, the main force was galloping towards the causeway leading to the main gates blowing horns. The Normans deliberately stopped some distance from the castle walls on the causeway. The tide was rising fast. Inside the abbey the monks had heard the commotion outside, but in the mist could not quite make out the size of the approaching force.

While the knights set about erecting a campsite as if planning a siege, William was approaching the north side of the Abbey. He whispered to his three companions. "I recollect an entrance below the ramparts by the rocks. It was used to give direct access to the sea. From there we can climb right up into the sanctuary."

Finding a rocky inlet they guided the boat between the rocks and moored it to an iron post hammered into the side of the rock. As they clambered out, William noticed another small boat moored nearby. The four knights silently climbed to the base of the wall until they reached a small wooden door at the bottom of the ramparts. It was locked and far too heavy to force.

"Damn it," said William, obliged to contemplate his next move. After several minutes a sound could be heard coming from within. They flattened themselves against the wall each side of the door. The sound of footsteps grew louder until they heard a key turn and the door open. An armed knight stepped out and William recognized Conan.

Conan had been congratulating himself on his shrewdness in keeping a boat hidden as a means to make his escape from the abbey if needed. However, as he moved towards the narrow rocky ledge, the last thing he would have expected was to be grabbed by two knights and pressed up against the wall. He froze as he recognized the Duke of Normandy.

"Ah, Conan, not planning another foray on Norman soil, are you? Harold, meet our illustrious neighbour from Brittany who chooses to greet us in such strange circumstances."

Still looking at Conan, William pointed to Harold. "Conan, let me introduce you to Earl Harold from England."

Conan looked terrified as William approached him, his sword pointing at his throat.

"Don't worry. I do not intend to splatter the walls of the Abbey with your blood."

William barked orders to his men. "Take him away. We will decide his fate later."

Conan offered no resistance while the knights tied his hands and guided him down to the boat. William turned to Harold.

"See how justly I deal with those that oppose me. Come let us return to Caen. You have done enough to warrant a knighthood."

Harold looked thoughtful as William strolled past him and clambered down to the boat. Before boarding he stopped and listened. There was no sound from the causeway. Having retrieved their horses, William sent one knight to break the news of Conan's capture to his troops camped outside the main gates of the abbey with orders to return to Caen, and another to the Abbott to express his regrets for the inconvenience.

After returning to Caen and imprisoning Conan in the dungeon, in the depths of the keep, William invited Harold to his chamber. He offered him a seat so that they were facing each other. They both knew that the friendship that had developed between them would now be put to the test. The months of hunting and feasting were over. It was now the moment of truth. Harold held a Norman helmet in his hands.

"I appreciate your generosity in bestowing upon me the title of a knight. It is an honour and I will covet this helmet. But I must soon return to England. Edward is ailing and I have learnt that in my absence my brother Tostig has turned against me.

He may seek refuge with King Harold Hardrada of Norway."

"To what purpose?" enquired William, raising his voice. "Do you not know that Edward made a promise to me years ago that I would succeed him. Come Harold. The time for games is over."

"I believe that he once mentioned it to my father," replied Harold, on the defensive. William stood up to give himself a more dominant position.

"What would you say to King William of England?"

Harold had to look up at William but attempted to avoid a direct reply.

"Edward has Norman blood and I cannot deny a certain legitimacy of your claim. But if Hardrada also seeks the throne for himself..."

William cut him short.

"And what of yourself. After all, your sister is Queen and you Saxons are a powerful force. Edward has already conveyed upon you considerable powers."

"True, my sister is Queen. But I have no clear blood line to the succession."

William took Harold's shoulders in his hands and stared into his eyes.

"Then swear allegiance to me. These past few months together we have made a good team. I will ask Matilda's sister Judith to contact Tostig and warn him not to join Hardrada. We can ensure that he will never become King. Swear it now and return to England as my vassal. Together, we can forge a powerful alliance."

William's aggressive stance had taken Harold by surprise.

"I don't know what to say. I need time to think."

William did not give him time. "I have made you a knight. You have seen my daughter Edwige. She is still a child but I promise her to you as your future wife. I will also release your kinsmen. But you must give me your word before your return to England."

William paused for a moment. "We leave for Bayeux immediately."

Without another word, William left the chamber. Outside, two Saxon housecarls were waiting. William gestured to them to enter. Their expression froze as Harold explained the Duke's proposal to them. One of the housecarls plucked up enough courage to speak his mind. "My Lord, are you going to accept such a proposition?" Harold started to pace up and down.

"If I do not so swear, William will not release my kinsmen and may use my refusal as an excuse to keep me here. As his guest? Or perhaps I will be another hostage?"

He stood still and looked at the housecarls.

"Would giving my oath to a Norman in a foreign land be sacred? I think not. I am a Saxon. The crown is not mine to pledge."

The housecarls glanced at each other as Harold looked out of the window and up at the sky. Dark clouds were gathering.

William had chosen Bayeux castle as the most suitable venue for Harold to take the vows. He had dressed himself in his formal robes and was seated on the throne surrounded by his most loyal barons. Harold gazed around the hall at the men facing him. Despite his age, Roger was, as ever, by William's side. William's brother Robert, William Fitzosbern, Roger de Montgomery and Walter Giffard stood either side of the throne. Odo, Bishop of Bayeux and Bishop Lanfranc, in their clerical robes were standing by the two altars. Harold saw that one was covered with a gold decorative fabric on which there was placed a prayer book. The altars had been positioned in the centre of the chamber, one on each side of the throne.

Alone amongst the Normans, Harold tried not to feel intimidated. He stood before the assembled dignitaries sensing the eyes fixed on him. William leaned forward towards Harold and spoke in a solemn manner.

"Have you reached a decision?"

Harold looked William in the eyes.

"I am prepared to agree with your wishes. I will swear."

There was a murmur in the hall as Harold was asked to place himself between the two altars. Lanfranc guided Harold's arms so that they were over the altars.

"If that is your true wish you must place your hands here."

Harold understood what he had to do and placed his right hand on the prayer book, while everyone watched and waited in anticipation. Hesitating, he then slowly lowered his left hand onto the other altar. Then he spoke quietly but assuredly.

"I, Earl Harold of Wessex, son of Godwin, do pledge under oath my allegiance to William Duke of Normandy and accept his right to succeed the sovereign King Edward as the rightful King of England."

After he had uttered his vow the hall was silent for a moment. Lanfranc stepped forward and taking the corner of the cloth in his hand, pulled away the cover. Harold's eyes widened and he stepped back shaken. He had not seen the sacred relics on which he had taken his vow; the ancient sacred bones of St Rasilphe and St Raven, which William had carefully hidden.

Only then did he begin to appreciate the magnitude of what he had done. He had taken a holy vow, sworn under oath, that Duke William, a Norman, would succeed King Edward and take the crown of England, which he had always coveted. It had been a carefully executed plan and he had fallen into the trap, deceived in a way he could never have envisaged. At that point nobody present could have imagined the consequences that would result from pronouncing a simple oath.

CHAPTER 32

News of Conan's escape from Caen reached William at Dieppe at the same moment as, under a cloudy sky, he was watching Harold's vessel riding the waves as it headed out of the natural harbour to the open sea towards England. Conan had taken advantage of William's absence and with the help of some Breton soldiers, overpowered the guards, stolen horses from the stables and succeeded in leaving the castle.

By the time William returned, Conan had reached the safety of his lands in Brittany where, after mustering his forces, he besieged the fortress at Dol. However, he had not reckoned on Count Ruallon, an ally of the Duke, being able to get a messenger through the blockade to warn William.

William personally led his army back to Brittany but before they could engage in conflict, Conan fled with his troops, this time taking refuge in the town of Dinan. Not content with relieving Dol, with Ruallon's support, William unrelentingly pursued Conan across Brittany and laid siege to Dinan. Faced by a much stronger force, and under the threat of being burned out, Conan finally capitulated and surrendered to the Duke, thus putting an end to his ambitions and the revolt in the west.

CHAPTER 33

The Saxon Chronicles:
"In this year was consecrated the minster at Westminster on childer mass day.

And King Edward died on the eve of the twelfth day and he was buried on the twelfth day within the newly consecrated church at Westminster."

When Harold returned to England he took with him an understanding of Norman culture and an insight into its military power. Apart from a highly mobile and disciplined mounted army, unheard of in Saxon England, which had emerged victorious in every conflict with his warmongering neighbours, William had introduced one of the most efficient administrative, legal and ecclesiastical regimes the world had seen since the Roman Empire. Based on Feudalism, Normandy was divided into fiefs, each under the control of barons, vassals to the Duke, who himself was a vassal to the King of France. The barons held tenure over their lands and exercised power over their serfs. Art and architecture flourished, as witnessed by the numerous castles, cathedrals, abbeys and churches that had been built throughout the Duchy. Normandy's monasteries were at the forefront of religious education and reform and the rule of law and justice became a pillar of the feudal society. Even in the secure confines of his own country Harold had good reason to be wary of the Duke of Normandy.

In December 1065, London was cold and damp. More than a year had passed since Harold had left. With his brother and nephew now free, he had gone to Westminster Palace to report to the King immediately. He was greeted by his sister, Queen Edith, who was relieved to see her brother back after such a long absence. They embraced each other.

"You have returned at last. I was becoming worried. So long without news."

"Edward wanted me to learn about the Duke of Normandy. Well, I have."

Edith interrupted him. "Before you tell me about your sojourn I must warn you that Edward is weakening?"

"That will change our plans," said Harold, not altogether surprised to hear of the King's ailing health. He had been aware that Edward was unwell before he had embarked on his journey.

"I obtained Wulfnoth and Hakon's release but I fear William has ambitions to expand Norman domination and, without a clear successor to Edward, he has this Kingdom in mind. Have you news of Tostig?"

Edith frowned. "Not since he left for Northumbria."

"And what of Hardrada?"

"Hardrada? I only know that the King is dying. I must go to him. You must also see him. He will want news of your journey."

Queen Edith and Harold made their way to the King's bedchamber. King Edward was lying in bed, his head propped up on a pillow. Archbishop Stigand, Robert of Jumieges, who had made the journey from Normandy, and a priest were by his side, comforting him. He smiled and raised an arm as Harold approached the bed. Harold was shocked to notice the change in The King's appearance. Edward looked thin and pale.

His voice had also grown weaker. "Harold. You are back. Have you seen my abbey? It is so near to completion but it seems God has chosen to take me to him before my life's work is finished. Promise... promise me that you and Edith will consecrate the abbey and that I will be laid to rest in its sanctuary."

Harold took the King's hand. "I give you my word Sire. I was too long in Normandy. I learnt a great deal about William and there were many things that had to be done. He finally agreed to release Hakon and Wulfnoth, who returned with me."

Edward nodded with satisfaction.

"I knew my cousin would be just. Did William talk about the future of England after I have passed on?"

Harold paused, gritting his teeth.

"No sire, he never made his aims clear, other than wishing that you regain your health." Harold looked apprehensively at the Queen as he spoke.

A few days later, from his bedchamber, the King heard bells ring out. His abbey was being consecrated by Archbishop Stigand in the presence of the Witan and other eminent Saxon nobles, while outside, crowds jostled and waited in the cold. They must have expressed concern that their King was not present. In his chamber Edward lay back, smiled and closed his eyes. After more than ten years of sweat and toil the building of his monumental abbey was finally complete. His life's ambition had been achieved. When the consecration ceremony was over, Queen Edith and Harold returned to the Palace and waited patiently in an antechamber to be summoned. They looked up as the priest opened the door to the King's chamber.

"The King is worsening. You must come now before it is too late."

They entered the bedchamber to see Edward on his deathbed. Archbishop Stigand, Robert of Jumieges and several dignitaries were gathered around the King.

Edith whispered to the Priest. "Has he named anyone yet?"

"Not a single word has emerged from his lips. Wait, he is trying to speak."

Edward slowly opened his eyes and recognized Harold, beckoning him closer.

"I heard the bells. My abbey has been consecrated. My life's work is done. Now I have so little time left, all I ask is that you, Harold, and my dear friend Robert resolve your differences. Promise me that Normans and Saxons will live together in peace."

Harold and Robert looked at each other expressing doubt in their eyes that the King's wish would ever be fulfilled.

"Harold, the country needs a strong hand at the helm and you, the Queen's brother, must look after her when I am gone."

With difficulty he held out his hand to Harold who grasped it.

"I commend this woman and all the kingdom to your protection. Remember that she is your lady and sister and serve her faithfully and do not take away from her any honour that I have granted her."

Having pronounced what was his last wish, Edward sighed and sank back in his bed. Robert appeared stunned by Edward's dying words and looked at Harold and Stigand. Their faces showed no sign of sadness or remorse. The priest turned to each of them in turn.

"Leave him in peace now, please."

It was apparent that the end was near. Without saying more they abided by the priest's request and slowly shuffled out of the bedchamber. As the door closed behind them, they could hear the priest giving the last rights to King Edward the Confessor.

CHAPTER 34

The Saxon Chronicles
*"Here Edward King of Angles lord sent his stedfast soul to
Christ. In the kingdom of God a holy spirit. He in the world
here abode while in the kingly throng of council sage. Four and
twenty winters wielding the sceptre freely wealth he dispensed.*
    *Then came forth free in his chambers in royal array good,
pure and mild Edward the noble, by his country defended – by
land and people, Until suddenly came the bitter death and the
king so dear, snatched from the earth.*
    Angels carried his soul sincere into the light of Heaven."

At midnight on a chilly night, made even colder by a bitter,
northerly wind, the year of our Lord 1065 expired and the year
1066 began; a year that would change the course of English
history. The 5th of January dawned cloudy and cold as the
sound of bells rang out across London to announce the death
of King Edward. Harold immediately summoned the Witan
and the following day the sixty most powerful Saxon Earls and
Bishops in the country held court at the Palace.

If anyone was aware of the weakness of William's claim to the
throne it was Harold. Although nobody could dispute the
Norman's royal bloodline, being born out of wedlock discred-
ited him in the eyes of the church. In any event this was
England, not Normandy. The Witan held the power to choose
the monarch. And the Witan had chosen Harold.
    "You all witnessed the King's dying wish that it is I who
should succeed him. The King will be buried according to his
last request in Westminster Abbey and I will take the crown
that Edward has proffered on me. If there is no one in this room
who opposes the King's word…" Harold looked around at the
assembled nobles. Nobody spoke out. He thought for a

moment, aware of the importance of what he was about to do. "Then, with your unanimous support I proclaim myself, Harold II, King of England."

He raised his arm and sword.

A crowd had gathered, lining the streets as King Edward's funeral cortege, with eight bearers carrying the oak coffin, slowly made its way from the Palace to the new Abbey by the river. Inside the Abbey, Saxon nobles filled the aisles as the coffin was carried slowly down the nave to the altar where it was carefully set down. Archbishop Stigand gave a blessing and Edward the Confessor was laid to rest, as he had always wished, in the Abbey that he had conceived and built on the banks of the river Thames, at the place called West Minster.

CHAPTER 35

The Saxon Chronicles:
"But the prudent king had settled the Realm on high born men – on Harold himself the noble Earl, who in every season faithfully heard and obeyed his Lord, in word and deed, nor gave to any what might be wanted by the Nation's King.

And Harold the Earl succeeded to the Kingdom of England, even as the king had granted it to him and men also had chosen him thereto and he was crowned a king on the twelfth day.

This year died King Edward and Harold the Earl succeeded to the Kingdom and held it for forty weeks and one day."

Without proclaiming a period of mourning, Harold had decided that his coronation could not wait. He was in no doubt that his rival across the sea in Normandy would contest his right to rule England. Whatever his reaction it would be too late. Despite having just presided over the burial of the King, Archbishop Stigand and the Witan were once again summoned to the Abbey. Dressed in royal robes, Harold knelt before the Archbishop. By his side, a priest held the sword of state and crown. Taking them from him, Archbishop Stigand raised his hands in ceremonial gesture, holding aloft the crown of England.

"With the powers bestowed upon me as Archbishop of Canterbury I abide by the dying wish of King Edward, for Earl Harold, son of Godwin, to succeed him." Taking the sword of state he handed it to Harold.

"In the name of the Lord, I proclaim you King. Arise Harold II, King of England."

In the full knowledge that Harold's coronation would never obtain papal sanction, Stigand proceeded to place the crown on Harold's head. It was to be his last ceremonial act. As chaplain and advisor to the Kings of England for almost half a century, he would also be the last Saxon Archbishop of Canterbury.

Duly crowned, Harold turned towards the assembled nobles, who all bowed before him. He was finally King, the most powerful man in the country. Yet despite having achieved everything his father had desired, his expression was not that of a man who had reached the pinnacle of success; he could not eliminate from his mind his vow at Bayeux and the reaction of the Duke of Normandy that he knew would inevitably result in conflict. He thought back to the night at Cerisy and the game of chess. William's words echoed in his mind. "Only one of us will be King."

PART V

CHAPTER 36

It was a sunny, crisp, winter morning in Normandy. William had moved his ducal court to a new palace at Rouen, on the banks of the Seine some fifty kilometres from the sea, where the river twisted and turned, winding its way in serpent fashion through the forests of upper Normandy.

He had left the palace early with a hunting party. In the calm of the woodlands sound travelled. At one point they halted and turned in their saddles, certain they could hear a horse approaching. A knight appeared out of the trees galloping towards them. He rode straight towards William bringing his horse to a halt by his side. He was breathless.

"Sire, we have news from England. King Edward is dead.

"Edward dead! William looked down for a moment. "May he rest in peace."

"And Earl Harold has taken the crown for himself."

William's expression changed from sadness to astonishment. "That cannot be."

"It is the truth my Lord," said the knight, recovering his poise. "They say the King appointed him as his successor before he died."

William turned his horse in a full circle.

"I must return to Rouen to consider this treachery."

He turned to the knight.

"Locate my brothers, Robert and Bishop Odo and ask that they make haste to join me there."

CHAPTER 37

Tostig had accepted his brother's coronation with resignation. As Earl of Northumbria, a title bestowed upon him by King Edward following the death of Siward in 1055, he had been away from the seat of power for ten years. But he had angered the Thegns and people of the north of England by his tyrannical rule and abuse of power. In 1065 King Edward had been obliged to take action and asked Harold to resolve the crisis. But the Thegns were adamant in their demands to remove Tostig and Harold had to capitulate and accept the nomination of Morcar of Mercia, who was appointed in his place.

Morcar and his brother Edwin had become Earls of Mercia after the death of their father Alfgar, son of Leofric, a loyal friend of Godwin. To ensure their future military and political support, Harold had abandoned Edith Swanneck, his long-standing companion, and married Leofric's daughter, who, as it happened, was also called Edith. Edwin and Morcar, therefore, became Harold's kinsmen and now one of them had been awarded all the estates that Tostig considered belonged to him by right. Tostig was banished and went to Flanders with his wife Judith. He would never forgive his brother. In his mind there had been a plot hatched against him. From that moment, he thought of nothing but revenge.

CHAPTER 38

Stunned by the news from England, William immediately returned to his palace at Rouen, where later that day he was joined by his brothers, companions and Norman barons for a crisis meeting. They were about to begin when a servant announced the arrival of Robert of Jumieges who had just returned from England, where he had witnessed Edward's death as well as being present at Harold's coronation. William embraced him, eager to learn about the situation in England.

"Robert, welcome back. Your timing could not have been more appropriate. What happened?"

Robert was offered a chair and sat down observing his fellow Normans around the table. "Edward could not survive the winter. I was with him when he was given the last rights."

"And Harold?" asked William.

"Edward's mind had deteriorated. I was at his side when he chose Harold to succeed him. There was not even time for mourning. Harold was crowned by Stigand as soon as Edward's body had been laid to rest."

Everybody around the table saw the menacing look on William's face.

"That's impossible. Edward gave a promise to me. And Harold swore under oath - on sacred relics." William was silent for a moment.

"And the Abbey?"

"Consecrated. Just before Edward died. His tomb is in the Abbey."

"So he accomplished his mission," said William glancing out of the window and pausing for a few seconds. "Now I will accomplish mine."

William began to pace up and down in no mood for frivolity, gesticulating as he spoke.

"Someone must go to England and warn Harold of his folly. His position is untenable. Inform Lanfranc so that he can advise the Pope of this blasphemous act and obtain papal support to take whatever steps are necessary to remove Harold. I must have the Pope's authority if I am to be the rightful King of England."

As the older statesman, Roger had been around long enough to sense the options swirling around William's brain.

"Think William, this is not an assault on a Norman castle. You are talking about invading a foreign country."

His brother, Robert, concurred with Roger. "Is this wise? You rule Normandy, but it is a mere province compared to England. You will have to face Saxons, Celts and Vikings."

"It is a matter of principle."

"Are principles worth dying for?" queried Odo, hoping to restrain his brother's growing frustration.

Odo's comment seemed to calm William.

"Interesting argument, you'd better take it up with God."

"Anyway, Stigand has no authority to appoint anyone, least of all a King. And Harold is a perjurer," asserted Odo. "His crown means nothing."

"Then he can renounce it and there will be no conflict," answered William curtly. "But don't imagine for one moment that power concedes."

"We have noticed that," said William Fitzosbern, rather courageously. William glared at his friend but remained silent.

"If I may voice my opinion..."

"I haven't asked for it."

William Fitzosbern was taken back by William's cutting reply.

"Well I am going to tell you anyway. For years we have fought costly battles to unite Normandy. Attack England? It's insane, too ambitious."

"Never say that. Not to my face." William was becoming angry. "I will not stand back and allow this Saxon to defy God."

"God or you?" questioned Odo, only to receive another icy stare from his brother, who was becoming more agitated at the criticism directed against him.

"You realise that Harold is trying to provoke you," said Roger. "He has an army protecting the south coast."

"Then he has succeeded," retorted William. "We must prepare to invade England."

"You think you can persuade the army to follow you," said William Fitzosbern.

"They will," replied William assuredly. "It is God's will."

William placed his hand on Roger's shoulder.

"I was born for this task. If I united Normandy, I can unite England."

He turned and addressed the assembled barons who, although still not entirely convinced, dared not oppose their Duke.

"I will not lose the opportunity that God has placed before me. Cut down trees to build ships. Flanders and Brittany have fleets of vessels. We will negotiate the purchase of every ship they can spare, requisition them if need be. Prepare arms, stock provisions and round up all the men and horses we can find. Emissaries must be sent to every corner of Normandy, Brittany, Flanders, Maine and France, to bring here all worthy fighting men who are prepared to serve our just cause."

Breathing heavily, he sat down on his throne with his hand on his chin.

"Dives!" he exclaimed. "We will set up our camp at Dives. The coast is protected there and when the wind turns it will favour reaching England. There is much work to do so let us not waste more time. I will set up my quarters at Troarn Abbey and bring my family to reside at Bonneville castle."

William thought for a moment. "But first I have a duty to fulfil."

It was the 18th June 1066. After his marriage William had kept his promise to the Pope and ordered the construction of two great abbeys in Caen. Odo had overseen the completion of the La Trinite Abbey, standing majestically on a hillside not far from the castle on the road to the coast. It had taken fourteen years to build. The twin symmetrical towers built with local grey stone flanked the central porch, beneath which were two massive doors. Crowds lined the street as William and Matilda, in ceremonial dress, rode towards the square where Lanfranc was waiting with Odo. As they dismounted to cheers, Lanfranc stepped forward to greet them.

"You earned the gratitude of his Eminence, Pope Nicolas, God rest his soul, for building the two abbeys."

"I gave my word did I not? It took six years for our marriage to obtain papal sanction. I regret Pope Nicolas did not live to see this day. We owe you our gratitude."

As William embraced Lanfranc he reminded himself of the debt he owed to his Italian advisor. Pope Nicolas had died in 1061 and Lanfranc's old student at Bec Hellouin, Anselmo, now Pope Alexander II, was in charge of the Pontificat. If papal blessing for the invasion of England had been obtained, it was due in no small measure to the close relationship that Lanfranc had established with the Pope. William's thoughts returned to the ceremony. Odo was trying to attract his attention.

"William, we are ready to consecrate the abbey."

William looked up at the twin towers.

"As it is the first to be consecrated I dedicate it for use as a convent. Matilda and I pledge our young daughter Cecily to this house of God."

He turned to Lanfranc.

"The Abbey of Saint Etienne shall become a monastery. When is completed I would like you to become Bishop.

"If that is your wish, I would be honoured."

Lanfranc could not refuse the Duke's generous offer, even though it would be several years before the Abbey of Saint Etienne, being built to the west of Caen, would be completed.

Odo was nudging William.

"Maurille, Archbishop of Rouen is here to preside over the ceremony."

William nodded and not wanting to delay the proceedings any longer, took Matilda by the arm. They entered the abbey of La Trinite to applause from the crowd and took their seats in the nave, looking around in admiration at the new house of God.

The most influential nobles and dignitaries of Norman society had been summoned to Caen. Acknowledging the distinguished guests, they could not fail to be proud of what they had achieved for the Christian church. As the Bishop started to pronounce his opening speech Matilda was nudging her husband. But he was paying little attention to the prayers. He was looking down at the cold, stone floor, his mind fixed on the task that confronted him, thinking of the men he would soon lead on the hazardous mission that would take them across the sea to England.

CHAPTER 39

In England another ruler was also looking at a stone floor. King Harold, seated on his throne in London, was deep in thought. He had received the emissary sent by Duke William and, after learning of the Norman's unacceptable conditions, asked him to return to convey his own message, which would leave William in no doubt that he had no intention of surrendering his title. If Harold seemed unperturbed by his reply, his brothers, Leofwine and Gyrth, could not disguise their unease. They had grown up in the shadow of their older brother but were now responsible landowners as well as able fighters.

"Are you sure you were right to ignore William's warning?" asked Leofwine. "When he learns of your refusal to accept his conditions, he will surely invade."

Harold did not bother to look up.

"Edward's dying wish was to proclaim me as his successor and I will not subject myself to the whims of the Normans. I gave his messenger my answer. I did indeed swear an oath. But how could I promise what I did not possess. The crown was not mine to give to anyone."

"But we know that a large fleet of vessels is being built on the coast of Normandy," exclaimed Gyrth. "It will not be long before the Normans will be ready to sail."

"If William attempts to invade England, the Saxon army on the coast will be waiting. We will push the Normans back into the sea."

"But what of Harold Hardrada?" Leofwine reminded his brother.

"Hardrada too believes he has a claim on English soil." added Gyrth. "He will surely invade Northumbria and then march south."

"Then I will give him just six feet of it," answered Harold, curtly.

Leofwine was studying a map. "If Hardrada does invade he must be stopped before he has time to move towards London. But how can we risk dividing our forces?"

Harold leaned back, considering his brother's comments. He was not wrong. There was a clear danger in splitting the Saxon army.

"I do not think it will be necessary to split our forces. William must first prepare a fleet of vessels and muster an army. Even the all-powerful Duke of Normandy cannot possibly complete such a task in less than three months. And to reach England he needs a favourable tide and wind. Morcar will not give up Northumbria without a fight. And he has Edwin with him. It gives us time to take the army to York and settle with the Vikings before the Normans ever set foot on English soil."

Harold had risen and was standing by the window as he spoke. Looking up to the heavens he saw a bright light streaking across the sky. His face could not conceal a growing unease about the events unfolding.

CHAPTER 40

The Saxon Chronicles:
"And in this year came William and won England. And in this year Christchurch Canterbury was burned.

  And this year appeared a comet on the fourteenth before the kalends of May."

Whatever Harold was planning, William was busy preparing for the invasion of England. The coast at Dives had been transformed into a gigantic, construction site. There were carpenters, tanners, blacksmiths, soldiers and peasants hard at work. Longships were being constructed with timber cut from the Norman forests. Weapons were forged and chain mail intricately pieced together. Branches were cut down, whittled and chiselled for bows and arrows, saddles were shaped and stitched, warehouses built to store the provisions gathered from the land, compounds erected to hold the horses and makeshift canteens set up to prepare meals. Nothing had been left unchecked, nothing ignored. To house his troops a vast camp had been erected. Despite the doubt that persisted among William's advisors and friends over the planned invasion, none contradicted the Duke's orders.

William Fitzosbern had been given the task of overseeing the operation and he and the Duke were constantly walking or riding around the site to supervise progress. One day as they toured the site he pulled William aside.

"Can I talk to you?" he remarked.

"Go ahead. What is it?"

"There is growing unrest among the men. They are tired of fighting and now this waiting…"

"You don't think they are occupied enough?"

195

"Many of us are concerned about the invasion."

"We have been through this already. Harold must be removed."

"Just so you can be King and prove something."

"What do I have to prove. Look around you. This is my destiny. If we are here it is God's will."

William nodded as he glanced around the huge campsite.

"Well, I promised the others to let you know what they think."

"Tell them not to think too hard. There is no turning back. Believe in God. Trust him. Trust me."

William Fitzosobern's thoughts returned to the task of preparation.

"We are short of horses and vessels and around 1000 men are still required."

The Duke slapped his friend on the shoulder.

"Then find them, find them." Go to Maine, Brittany and Poitiers, even France if you have to. Thanks to Lanfranc the Pope has given us his blessing. This is now a Holy War and the prize is England. That must surely be sufficient incentive to entice some of our adventurous neighbours to join us in this mission."

They stopped to look at blacksmiths working on weapons in the temporary forge, erected on the shore. William took a sword and then a lance to test against armour.

"How are the swords shaping up?"

A blacksmith was pouring red hot metal into a mould. "They will be strong, Sire."

"Good. Keep working at it. We will need as many weapons as you can make. I want swords with fine edges, tough enough to parry the mightiest blows from Saxon axes."

William Fitzosbern felt another slap on his back as William tried to reassure him by acting in a more jovial manner. "Don't forget to supply each vessel with enough food for the voyage. And wine."

As they walked to the Duke's tent, William Fitzosbern glanced up at the sky.

"Look!"

William followed his gaze and saw a bright light streaking across the sky.

"That is God's sign. It can only be a good omen."

CHAPTER 41

William was so preoccupied with his preparations on the coast of Normandy that he had momentarily forgotten the situation in England. He was, therefore, surprised when it was announced that Harold's brother Tostig had arrived in Normandy and wished to see him. Although Tostig's marriage to Matilda's sister Judith had made him his brother in law, the two men had never met. Tostig had journeyed from his exile in Flanders with a bold proposal to offer his help in deposing Harold. William met Tostig at Troarn Abbey. Founded by his friend, Roger de Montgomery, it lay in a valley on the road to Dives and had become William's headquarters while preparing the invasion. William was dining at the table laid with bowls of fruit and wine when Tostig arrived.

"I bid you welcome. Join me."

William pointed to an empty bench seat with his knife. Tostig sat down and helped himself to some fruit. William observed his guest noticing that, while he was not as tall as Harold, with his long blond hair and moustache, the resemblance was evident.

"Is it not strange that we have never met. We are brothers in law through marriage yet I only know Harold. After months as my guest your brother and I came to understand each other well."

Taking two goblets, William poured some wine for Tostig and then for himself.

"What Harold did is unpardonable. Both to me and the church."

Tostig put down his goblet sharply. "Harold is not your family. He humiliated me. That is why I come to offer you my support. I have an army ready to sail to Northumbria to recover my lands. It would create a second front in the North when you invade."

"Invade. Who says I am going to invade?" William was stuffing food into his mouth as he spoke.

Tostig sat back and smiled. It would have been difficult for William to conceal his intentions with all the construction work taking place.

William listened thoughtfully to Tostig's plan and did not seek to delve into his reasons for turning against his brother. That was a personal matter. William was only concerned about his own mission. The Normans were still not ready to set sail and, while William could appreciate the strategic merits of an ally in the north of England, while he would be landing in the south, the reality was that Morcar still controlled Northumbria. Tostig could offer no firm guarantees. And could he be trusted? Without committing himself he nevertheless did nothing to dissuade Harold's brother from pursuing his objectives.

Taking advantage of the last favourable winds before the summer season, Tostig sailed to England with the rebel Saxon soldiers that had accompanied him to Normandy. A raiding incursion on the Isle of Wight to find provisions had led to the destruction of some villages, news of which would quickly reach King Harold. He then continued along the coast to Sandwich where he consolidated his forces. After passing Dover Castle under the cover of night, Tostig's fleet, now comprising sixty ships, sailed north towards the Humber. However, Morcar, with a much larger force, had learnt of the approaching fleet. When Tostig landed and moved inland, Morcar was prepared and successfully repelled the invasion. Tostig was forced to abandon his attempts to reclaim Northumbria and took a decision, which was to seal his fate, and that of England.

Retreating to his fleet anchored near the mouth of the Ouse, Tostig ordered his troops to find a safe haven further along the coast while he would cross the North Sea to Norway. His plan was to seek the help of the only other person prepared to stand in the way of both Harold and William in their claim for the English crown: Harald Hardrada, the last Viking King.

After reaching the Norwegian coast dotted with its multitude of islands and inlets, Tostig manoeuvred his vessel into a deep water Fjord. With his tiny vessel dwarfed by the sheer cliffs towering above him, he sailed cautiously into the heart of Hardrada's realm. Tostig was sitting back reflecting on the silence and flat calm, icy water when suddenly from behind a bend three longships appeared. With over thirty oars rising and splashing in unison in each vessel, they bore down so swiftly he had no time to turn and run. Overpowered, he and his crew had no choice but to accompany the Viking longships until they reached a village where other vessels were moored. While his men were confined to the ship, Tostig was led through the village by his Viking guardians to the general surprise of the inhabitants, unaccustomed to seeing foreigners in their midst. They reached a large hut in the village square and Tostig was pushed inside. At the far end of a large wooden bench table, a group of men were drinking and laughing.

As Tostig entered they looked up and several pairs of Viking eyes scoured at the stranger who had interrupted them. One stood up and moved closer. With a reputation as a formidable warrior in the pure Viking tradition, nearly two metres tall, with blue eyes, blond hair and a thick moustache hiding a tough, scarred face, he had earned his name; Hardrada meant 'Hard Ruler'.

After listening to his unwelcome guest there was little reason for Hardrada not to accept Tostig's proposal. He had nurtured an ambition to take the crown of England ever since he had succeeded to the throne of Norway in 1047, when he was thirty-one, after the premature death of his nephew Magnus. If Edward had died without an heir, Hardrada's claim to the English throne was based on his Viking bloodline and a vague promise supposedly given to Magnus by Cnut's eldest son and successor, Hardicanute. Neither the Normans nor the Saxons could dispute his right. He was now fifty years old. He would take the crown and the Vikings would once again rule England.

Tostig was relieved to be invited to join Hardrada's table. Later, sufficiently inebriated, he was allowed to wander off unescorted. Taking a path through the village he noticed a young maiden, her blue eyes and blond hair, attracting his attention. She was having difficulty carrying a heavy cauldron uphill. He gestured to her and with a large smile she allowed him to take it from her, pointing to a cottage close by. When they reached the door she took Tostig's arm and pulled him towards her. Tostig lowered the cauldron, placing it near the door and politely stepped back. She was insisting, almost dragging him inside. Tostig resisted thinking of Judith back home. But would he ever see her again? Looking around to see if anyone was watching, Tostig took a deep breath and stepped inside the cottage carefully shutting the door behind him.

CHAPTER 42

With Tostig gone, William pursued his preparations in Normandy. He had called his barons to a meeting at Troarn. They were standing around a table on which there was a map of Normandy and southern England. William laid his sword on one side to keep it flat, holding down the other edge with his hand.

"You all saw the omen in the sky. It is a sign. We know that Tostig is on his way to Hardrada. Harold cannot ignore their threat and must meet them somewhere."

He was poking his finger at England's south coast.

"When can we be ready? If we can invade while his army is far away...

Roger de Montgomery interrupted.

"We need at least another two weeks. Then it depends on the wind."

William thumped the table.

"The wind, always the wind. Listen. I have been thinking. We will sail the fleet to St Valery. The estuary is wide and well protected and the distance to England, shorter. It will also test our ships and give the men some action. We will wait there for a favourable wind."

William looked around expecting a response but none was forthcoming.

"What fate! The north wind that keeps us here favours Hardrada's longships crossing from Norway."

CHAPTER 43

The Saxon Chronicles:
"There was slain Harald, the fair hair'd King of Norway and Earl Tostig, and a multitude of people with them both Norsemen and English"

William was correct. Hardrada had needed little encouragement from Tostig to assemble a fleet. Whatever he thought of Harold's brother or his Saxon followers, Hardrada was not going to lose the opportunity that Tostig's arrival had provided. The northerly winds had continued to blow and on the 18th September 1066 at the head of a fleet of three hundred longships filled with Viking warriors, Hardrada and Tostig reached the north east coast of England and sailed up the Humber to the river Ouse, where Tostig's army was camped.

"We are almost there," said Tostig pointing to the smoke from his camp in the distance rising above the trees lining the riverbank. Hardrada instinctively put his hand on the hilt of his sword. "I hope your soldiers know we are with you. I do not want Saxon blood on Viking swords, at least not yet."

Tostig gave him a cautious stare. "If we are to accomplish our mission we must stand together. Once Northumbria is mine again I will leave you to claim the throne of England."

Reaching the camp, the drakkars anchored, tied together side by side three deep along the shore, and the Vikings disembarked. Putting aside their differences the two armies spent the night rather warily, side by side, and by morning they were ready to advance to face Edwin and Morcar.

The two Saxon earls had been warned of the Viking fleet and had little choice but to face the challenge. The sight of hundreds of Viking longships sailing up river had terrified the peasants whose villages lay close to the bank and the news had reached them quickly. The Saxon army blocked their path near York, but they were no match for a far superior force and in a bloody encounter at Gate Fulford, the Saxons were put to the sword by the invaders. Hardrada and Tostig then confidently stormed across the north with their combined army of Vikings and Saxons, taking York before coming to a halt on the banks of the Derwent river at a site called Stamford Bridge, where they established a campsite. Tostig had returned. The first part of his plan had succeeded. Northumbria belonged to him once again.

Unknown to them, that same afternoon, Harold's Saxon army was resting not far from York after a long and arduous march from London. Despite Gyrth and Leofwine's reservations, Harold had taken the decision to dismantle his defences along the south coast and recall all his soldiers to counter the threat from the Norsemen. After his forces had regrouped in London, they had taken less than five days to march two hundred miles to reach York and make their camp.

Harold was in his tent discussing tactics with Gyrth and Leofwine when the flap opened and a soldier entered.

"Sire, we bring news that Tostig and Hardrada are camped a few miles down river at Stamford Bridge with their armies."

Harold sat shaking his head in disbelief.

"I have tried to put thoughts of Tostig's treachery from my mind. He never accepted Morcar taking his land. But I would never have believed he would take arms against his own family."

"They cannot know we are here," said Gyrth, hoping his assumption was correct.

Leofwine looked at Harold.

"If we strike early tomorrow the surprise could be to our advantage."

Harold nodded. "You are right. Let the soldiers rest now and order them to rise before daybreak. They must be prepared for an attack as soon as dawn breaks."

Placing guards on night duty around the camp, Harold and his brothers made sure that their orders had been conveyed to the soldiers, before taking a light meal and then retiring to bed themselves. They rose before dawn and made their way to a hill overlooking the enemy. Fires were still burning. They could make out the camp, which extended to both sides of the river.

"There is little movement," observed Gyrth.

"So it appears," remarked Harold. "But they are spread over both banks of the river and there is but a single bridge."

"Let us hope they will still be asleep when we attack," said Leofwine.

"I wonder where Tostig and Hardrada are," muttered Harold.

Under cover of darkness, they returned as silently as possible to their camp.

Tostig and Hardrada were both asleep in their tents. Believing that the defeat of Morcar and Edwin had secured their control of the North they had not for one moment considered the possibility that the Saxon army led by Harold had already reached the banks of the Derwent and was ready to strike.

As dawn broke on the 25th September, the soldiers, who were huddled in their tents, could feel that it was going to be a chilly day. Housecarls passed through the camp to wake up the troops who dressed and armed themselves without speaking. Word was passed from tent to tent. "Keep as quiet as possible."

In almost total silence the Saxon army gathered in columns and advanced through the forest towards the Vikings before coming to a halt about one hundred metres from the enemy camp. Hidden by the thick undergrowth, the housecarls took up their positions at the front.

"It looks quiet, don't it?" muttered a soldier to his nearest companion. The soldier turned to him noticing how young he looked.

"It won't be for long. Still it's better than doing nothing on the south coast."

The young soldier's name was Erwulf. Like many of Harold's housecarls, he was in his early twenties. He had been a Fyrd in his village, taking up arms when ordered to do so by the Earl of the Manor. As a Fyrd he had been used to fighting with scythes, slings and hayforks until he had been offered the chance to become a paid soldier – a housecarl. The months of training at Dover castle had been hard but now he had protective clothing and real weapons at his disposal. Over his leather undergarment he wore a suit of chain mail with a scabbard designed to carry his tempered steel sword, and carried a circular wood and leather shield. His girl, Ayla, had been impressed when he last returned to his village to see her and they planned to marry. All that waiting for an invasion on the south coast had been so tedious until the King had given orders for the army to move north. The journey had been tough on his feet. But now he thought about the battle ahead. He feared the Vikings. They had a reputation for being unmerciful in combat. This time, however, they were unprepared, or so he had been told. He patted the simple locket held by a string around his neck that Ayla had given to him as a good luck charm. It had been carved from wood and portrayed the head of a sheep.

His thoughts were interrupted by the voice of King Harold passing the order to advance. The ranks of Saxon housecarls moved forward in line armed with the feared double handed battle axes and maces that were so deadly in close combat. Holding their round shields, they formed a solid wall. Torches had been lit and as the line advanced it seemed like a solid wall of flame was on the march.

As they moved out of the line of trees across the open field they started to quicken their pace and began to shout. The noise spread panic. Caught by surprise, the Viking warriors were forced to abandon their tents half dressed. In battle the Vikings wore barbours made of hide covered with chain mail. But at night they removed the heavy cumbersome clothing. They were cut down before they had time to put on their battle dress or arm themselves. As Harold's men surged through the camp setting fire to tents and equipment, those Vikings who had escaped the carnage managed to regroup and retreat across the single wooden bridge spanning the river to join their comrades camped on the other bank.

As the last Vikings sped across, one warrior turned and stood his ground in the centre of the bridge, waving his battle axe and shouting at the Saxons. He must have been over two metres tall and was built like an oak tree. Single handed he slew all around him, preventing Harold's forces from crossing the river. One smart soldier, seeing what was happening, slid into a small craft tied to the bank and rowed out into the middle of the stream where the current edged him towards the bridge. In the turmoil of battle the Viking warrior had not noticed the boat or its occupant creeping towards him.

The soldier ducked his head as the boat swept beneath the bridge and brought it to a halt by quickly swinging a rope around a timber post. Taking his lance, the soldier forced it up through the gaps in the timber planks, striking the unsuspecting Viking in the buttocks and bringing him down. With a huge cry the Saxons then tore across the bridge, heaving the writhing body into the water where the current swept it away. Consolidating their position, they lined up behind their shields to face the Vikings, who had by now reassembled with Tostig's Saxon army to form their own solid defensive wall. Harold, Gyrth and Leofwine had watched the housecarls storm across the bridge from a distance.

"Have you seen Tostig or Hardrada anywhere," Harold asked his brothers as they marched across the bridge. They both shook their heads.

Hardrada and Tostig had camped on the far side of the river and had been spared from the initial carnage inflicted on their men. Although Harold's assault had taken them by surprise, the sacrifice of the Viking warrior on the bridge had given them time to don their chain mail and barbours and gather their weapons. They had now joined the ranks of soldiers who had regrouped and stood defiantly at the front of their forces, facing Harold's Saxons.

Moving forward in formation Harold's housecarls approached the Viking defensive line and, with a clash of steel, both armies began to push forward wielding their swords and axes. It was a matter of strength; whose line would break first in the hand to hand combat. Finally, outnumbered due to the loss of so many men, the Viking defensive wall was breached in the centre allowing the Saxons to force their way through. The Viking line collapsed and overpowered, the warriors took flight. Hardrada screamed at his retreating soldiers to stand their ground. They paid little heed to their King who, left to battle on with a handful of men, had no chance against rampant Saxons wielding battleaxes. It took five hits to the body and head before the Viking King fell to the ground. The battle was over. The Saxons pursued the Vikings to the river where they had moored their drakkars. No quarter was given, no Viking spared. Of the fleet of three hundred vessels only twenty five managed to escape, leaving the rest burning or sinking along the banks. Many of Tostig's Saxon troops surrendered to Harold's army but were spared the fate of their Viking comrades. Harold was not going to kill his own people because of his brother's treachery.

Tired and dirty, he began to enquire after his brother and the Viking King. He wandered around the battlefield, littered with bodies, searching in vain.

"Sire, we have found them. Hardrada is dead but your brother is alive...only just."

"Take me to him," said Harold to the housecarl who had brought him the news he had dreaded. Tostig was lying on his back in a ditch by the riverbank, his face covered with blood. He was still breathing, albeit with difficulty. Harold knelt next to him and gently turned him over, taking his head in his arms. He could see that his wounds were serious.

"I fear you are spent, Tostig. I should despise you for turning against your own family. What led you to go against me?"

Tostig was weakening. Despite the pain he forced himself to speak, pausing to catch his breath.

"Father always gave you what you asked. He wanted you to be King. I had to prove I could compete. You took away what was mine. Now you have the crown...and the Kingdom."

As he uttered his last words and his head arched back, Harold took him in his arms.

"You misunderstood my intentions. But it matters little now. I can only pray for your soul and forgive you, brother."

Harold gently lowered his body to the ground with the help of the housecarl.

"Bury him here in Northumbria. It is what he would have wished for. Now let me see Hardrada."

Hardrada's bloody corpse lay near the bridge, surrounded by the lifeless bodies of Viking soldiers that had died trying to protect their chief. Harold surveyed the scene and, looking down at the body, felt some remorse for the death of his Norwegian adversary. "He was a Viking warrior. I cannot deny him a Viking burial."

Late in the day with the sun setting, two funeral vessels, built from the remains of the Viking drakkars, were ready to receive the Saxon Earl and Viking monarch. Each had a small tent shaped, wooden burial chamber at the stern built from planks. Tostig's final resting place had been lowered into a pit dug by soldiers. Once the body had been laid inside the burial chamber, and various objects piled around it, the vessel was covered with earth leaving a large mound. It was the Saxon way.

In the other vessel, Hardrada's body, in full battle dress, was laid inside the chamber, his sword placed in one hand and laid across his chest. Clothes, helmets and items gathered from the battle site were placed around the body, together with drinking horns and eating utensils. Hardrada had died sword in hand. Valhalla would be waiting for him. At Harold's signal, soldiers eased the craft into the water and watched it miraculously slowly float downriver where it would finally drift into the bank, to be swallowed by tall reeds.

A year or so later the vessel was discovered and Hardrada's remains were shipped home to Trondheim to be placed in the tomb of the Norwegian Kings.

CHAPTER 44

Before embarking for St Valery, William had one last duty to fulfil. It had been years since he had last paid his respects to his mother. She had been buried in Grestain, just north of Bonneville and he had asked his brothers, Robert and Odo to accompany him to her tomb. Leaving the camp at Dives in the hands of William Fitzosbern and Roger of Montgomery, the journey took no more than two hours.

The chapel was small. Carrying torches, which threw up shadows on the walls, they descended the stone steps that led to the crypt. Inside, William and his brothers slowly advanced towards the simple stone tomb in which their mother, Arlette, had been laid to rest. They knelt down. After a few minutes of silent prayer, William gestured to his brothers to leave him alone and they returned to the chapel. William leaned forward, placed his hands on the tomb and looked up at the ceiling.

"Mother, by not taking the vows of marriage you could not have known the suffering I have had to endure. Perhaps if my father had not made peace with God while I was so young, things would have been different. For years I had to combat those who would not accept me and I reacted so harshly towards anyone who dared call me a bastard. After six years the Pope finally gave papal blessing to my marriage with Matilda and our children can grow up as true Christians, as I could not. I brought peace to Normandy and now face my greatest challenge; to take the crown of England. I am trapped in my destiny. I ask you to watch over me and protect Robert and Odo in this quest. Dominus Deus, defende nos in proelio."

William bent down, kissed the stone, took the torch in his hand and began to climb the steps back into the sunlight.

The voyage to St Valery was long and perilous. William had divided the fleet into groups leaving at hourly intervals. For fifty kilometres, the ships hugged the coast heading east towards the Seine estuary, protected from the northerly winds by the high cliffs, before turning northwards to Graville and rounding the cape to Fecamp.

From there the ships were faced with a ninety kilometre journey across the open sea. They maintained sight of land but were exposed to north easterly winds. The clouds had been gathering but gave no sign of the impending bad weather. The storm hit when the fleet was passing Fecamp. Despite all the planning, all the meticulous preparation, there was nothing William could do against the elements. He could only look on helplessly as the sea rose and wind howled. With no safe harbour to give them protection, the strong sea currents split the fleet, scattering the ships in all directions. Overloaded, some of the longships could not bear the extra weight of seawater pouring over the gunnels, flooding the deck. They capsized and sank, taking down with them soldiers, horses and provisions.

In the safety of the estuary at St Valery, William had time to reflect on the damage to his fleet and to his reputation. The last thing he wanted was to spread bad news, which might demoralize his army before the invasion proper began. He did his best to conceal the incident, unable himself to determine the exact number of casualties. Only those that had witnessed stricken vessels going down and the cry of drowning men, knew there had been some loss of life. It was a disaster, which did not bode well for the longer voyage, which would take them to England.

The estuary at St Valery was as just as William had described. A wide stretch of shallow water penetrating several kilometres inland bordered by flat marshland and protected from the sea. When the combined fleet dropped anchor, William withheld details of the missing ships and disclosed little information about the real loss of life. With no clear idea of how long they would have to wait and, to keep the troops occupied, orders were given to empty the vessels. For several days William's commanders directed the building of a new camp, a paddock for the horses and stocking of provisions. Poles and timbers were imbedded into the sand to support the vessels at low tide. It kept the men busy but having already erected and dismantled one camp at Dives the soldiers were wondering whether they would ever be ready to embark and some questioned whether it was all worthwhile.

September arrived. The weather was becoming cooler, the days shorter. William knew time was running out. They had to make the sea crossing before autumn gave way to winter. William could not afford to risk missing a change of wind. He gave his commanders the order they had been waiting for; the ships were to be loaded again and made ready to sail.

On the top of a dune overlooking the St Valery estuary William was sitting alone, his horse by his side, staring out towards the open sea, his eyes fixed on the horizon. Somewhere beyond, lay England. From time to time he wiped away the spray that streaked across his face.

Below, the beach was crowded with soldiers loading weapons and provisions and cajoling reluctant horses noisily up the specially built ramps. He was oblivious to the sound of approaching horses until Robert and Odo reached his side.

"Everything seems to be progressing according to schedule," announced Robert. "The loading should be completed by tomorrow. Then it depends on the wind."

William looked at him and up at the sky. He disliked the waiting, the uncertainty.

"We have been waiting for the wind to blow from the south for three weeks now. At least the rain has ceased."

"After these last months of preparation it is hard to believe that we are finally on our way to England."

Odo's voice expressed both relief and apprehensiveness that their quest was finally about to begin. William glanced towards the sea again.

"Each passing day makes Harold stronger and better prepared."

"We have to expect some resistance," said Odo. "He won't welcome you with open arms."

William took a last look out to sea, stood up and holding the reins, climbed into the saddle.

"I have been once to England. I was greeted as a friend. That I have to return in such circumstances pains me but Harold will not capitulate. He has the crown and intends to keep it."

"If only we knew what awaits us," said Robert, his voice expressing concern.

"Whatever awaits us, I can tell you now. Nothing that has gone before has been so daunting. Nothing that comes after will be so decisive."

Digging his heels into his horse's flank and followed by his brothers, William eased his mount down the slope.

With the tide still out the three riders trotted across the sands stopping from time to time to supervise the loading. William noticed Turold pulling a horse on board a vessel.

"Careful with the horses, we will need them in good shape in England. Our lives may well depend on our steeds."

When they reached his drakkar, the Mora, William stopped. Compared to the other ships the Mora was an impressive vessel; longer and wider. It could accommodate a larger number of troops and horses. The stern had been fitted out by Matilda with seating and cushions. A dragon's head had been carved on the bow, while at the stern there was a figure of a child with a bow and arrow primed and pointed towards England.

Odo looked with admiration at the vessel that was to convey him to England. It looked solid enough, he thought, apprehensive about making the sea crossing.

"Your drakkar certainly befits a Duke."

"Matilda persuaded her kinsmen to bring it here from Flanders," said William, slapping the stern with the palm of his hand. "She insisted on decorating it for the voyage. At least everyone will know where I can be found."

On reaching William's tent, they dismounted, tethered the horses and disappeared inside.

At that very moment a knight was sitting high in the saddle of his horse at the top of another ridge of the dunes observing with wonder the vast campsite filled with thousands of men going about their tasks, and the hundreds of ships anchored in the bay. He tugged on the reins and gently guided his mount down the slope and trotted along the beach, stopping only when he reached William's tent.

Inside, William and his brothers were huddled over a table looking at plans.

"I still wonder how you persuaded men from Brittany, Maine, Flanders and France to join us in such a venture," said Robert still overwhelmed by the number of longships, barges and the military force William had mobilised.

"You know," William answered, smiling, "The best way to keep peace with neighbours is to find a common enemy. We have one – England."

Their mirth was interrupted by the sound of the flap opening. The knight entered, removing his helmet.

"My Lord, I bring news from England. King Harold Hardrada of Norway has landed in the North of England and joined forces with Harold's brother Tostig. Harold has moved his entire army north to York to counter them."

William nodded approvingly. He had been waiting for news from his spies in England.

"Well, whatever the outcome it will remove one contender for the crown. If Harold has moved his whole army so far away in the north we have a good chance to reach

England without opposition. The sooner we leave the better."

William was not to know that four hundred miles north the outcome had already been decided.

A soldier suddenly entered the tent, waving his arms in excitement.

"Sire, the wind! I think the wind is turning."

They hurried out of the tent and looked up at the sky. Thick clouds had formed, breaking only to let specks of blue sky and the sun's rays pierce through. The clouds were heading north, ship's flags on the mast were bearing north flapping in the wind and the weather vane on the church was spinning, pointing towards the north. The southerly winds that William had been waiting for so patiently, had finally arrived.

Odo raised his hands and looked upwards.

"It is God's will. The wind has changed direction."

William slapped him on the back. "God has given us a sign. The time has come to set sail. I told you the comet was a good omen. Prepare the fleet to leave."

By the following morning the loading of the ships was almost complete. William rode the short distance to the castle at Eu taking Turold and Goles with him. Matilda and the children had accompanied Roger on the long journey from Bonneville and taken up residence. It was a fitting venue to bid farewell. Fifteen years had passed since they had taken the vows of marriage in the castle's chapel.

"Our preparations are over. The fleet is ready and the wind has finally turned. We leave for England with the evening tide."

Roger put his hand on William's shoulder.

"Take me with you to my last great battle."

William held Roger's hands, looking into the ageing face of his most loyal kinsman.

"You have been by my side and fought in too many battles. Everything I have learnt, you taught me. But now I go to

England I need to leave Normandy in trustworthy hands. None are more trustworthy than yours."

Roger shrugged his shoulders.

"I understand. I know you will come through as you have always come through. You have God on your side."

"I owe you more than I can repay," said William embracing Roger.

"I did nothing more than was expected of me, William. Your grandfather and your father dreamt that we Normans would one day rule England. God, it seems, has chosen you to realise their wish. Fulfil your destiny. That will be my recompense."

"The Courage or The Fear?" said William. Roger nodded appreciatively and they both smiled as they remembered his advice when William was a child.

William took Matilda's hand and looked at their four sons and four daughters.

"In my absence I entrust Normandy to you with the authority to rule as Regent in my name. Roger will be at your side."

He knelt down and embraced his children.

"My sons, you must learn to take responsibility. He took his eldest son, Robert, in his arms. One day, with God's blessing you will be a Duke and perhaps a King. Now you must look after your mother."

Matilda stood, arms folded, and gave William a cynical glance.

"There is nothing to worry about. Normandy will be here when you return."

William ignored her comment and took his daughters in his arms.

"And you, my daughters. You too must help your mother while I am away."

He kissed them. William turned to Goles who was chatting to Turold and placed a hand on his shoulder.

"Turold is coming with me to England, but I need you to stay here."

Turold and Goles looked at each other. "I will miss you," said Turold.

"Come back safely," replied Goles and the two hugged each other.

William turned to embrace Matilda.

"I am staying by your side until you leave."

William thought for a moment not sure whether to agree. Then he nodded.

"Come then. We must return to St Valery."

As William, Matilda and Turold rode off to join the fleet, Roger, with Goles by his side, watched them from the Ramparts. "I hope I am right about God being on his side," thought Roger aloud.

During his lifetime William had never lost a battle, imposing his will on his enemies in every conflict in which he had been engaged. But this was different. England was across the sea, and a much larger country. The crown was on the head of a powerful Saxon warrior who had the support of his people. Could the Norman invaders defeat the Saxons in battle in their own land? Would the Saxons be prepared to accept a Norman as their King? Roger could not conceal his apprehension.

CHAPTER 45

The ramps were serving their purpose on the shore at St Valery as the last of the vessels were being loaded with horses, provisions, and arms. It was confusing and noisy with men moving about, gesticulating, giving and taking orders, talking amongst themselves. By mid afternoon the vessels were fully laden and ready for the tide. William took up a position on the sand standing before a group of barons, while the soldiers who had all embarked watched from their vessels. William wondered if his voice would carry far enough. He raised his sword.

"All of you brave and worthy Normans, Bretons, Flemish, and Frenchmen, who sail with me this day must know that we fight a noble cause. King Edward, of Norman blood, once pledged that I was his rightful heir. The man now on the throne of England, Harold, reneged on a sacred oath he gave to me."

He pointed to England and then to the banner on top of the mast of the Mora. The white flag with a gold cross emblazoned in the centre was the Vexillium Sancti Pietri, or banner of St Peter.

"Our quest is not one of greed, vengeance or anger, but a Holy crusade, one of good against evil, which all God fearing men should pursue with honour. It is our duty as Christians to pursue this mission and we sail to England with the blessing of the Pope. We were given an omen in the sky and, with God's will, we will overthrow the tyrant who stole the crown of England and you will reap the rewards of victory."

The moment of truth had finally arrived. William looked out over the water at his fleet. More than four hundred and fifty longships were scattered across the estuary. They had been built, gifted from Flanders or purchased from Brittany and France. Except for the larger Mora, each vessel was twenty to twenty-five metres long and would take thirty oarsmen. Following Viking tradition, the prow and stern of each drakkar was sculptured with the head of a bird or animal. A single square, multicoloured sail held by rigging was ready to be hoisted to a sturdy oak mast, rising from the centre of the deck. Fixed to the stern on the starboard side, a heavy, thick timber oar, projecting deep into the water, would guide the vessel. Each ship could carry thirty to forty armed foot soldiers or a dozen horses with their knights. Ropes were attached to each horse with pulleys, tied to the ship's sides to protect them from any sudden movement caused by waves during the sea voyage. Some vessels, designed as transport carriers, had been commandeered from as far away as Aquitaine solely for provisions and, ignoring the lessons of the previous voyage, their decks were still loaded to the gunnels.

William's army consisted of more than five thousand men and two thousand knights and horses. Most had come from Normandy, Flanders, Brittany and France. But not all were loyal to William. Mercenaries from other parts of Christendom had joined the adventure attracted by tales of riches that lay on the other side of the sea.

Every ship had a crew of sailors and servants whose task was to attend to the provisions and horses. For what was going to be one of the greatest invasions ever undertaken, the Duke of Normandy had left nothing to chance. Only one thing eluded him; knowing what lay ahead at the end of the voyage. William stopped before boarding his vessel. Deep in thought, he looked down as the waves lapped his boots.

An elderly, blind soothsayer, who William had allowed to accompany the expedition, stepped towards the water's edge. He stooped to gather pebbles and threw them into the sea. Then he raised his arms to the sky.

"I look out and hear troubled waters. But I predict that the sea will calm and the south wind will blow. I foresee a safe crossing for all who make this voyage."

William listened in silence as the soothsayer spoke and then moved off quickly with his brothers to embark. The tide was beginning to come in. There was a grinding and splashing sound as one by one the vessels started to float, their wooden supports collapsing and floating away as the sea closed in.

William, at the stern of the Mora, took hold of his medallion and kissed it. Trumpets sounded as peasants' axes sliced through the ropes holding the ships and the armada prepared simultaneously to hoist the sails and slowly edge out towards the open sea. The voices of more than seven thousand soldiers could be heard cheering as the voyage began.

Night had fallen at sea. The water was calm except for a slight swell causing the vessels to roll. The crossing was quiet apart from the sound of waves striking the bows and the lanterns of four hundred and fifty vessels illuminating the sky. William walked along the deck of the Mora nodding to the knights who were huddled together. He checked that the horses, strapped up, were as comfortable as possible. For William, the horses were as important as his men. They would be nervous at sea and needed reassuring during the voyage.

As the hours passed with nothing to do, it provided an opportunity to rest. William, Odo and Robert, sat at the stern able to lie back on the cushions that Matilda had provided to make the journey less uncomfortable. It was going to be a long night. They could sleep and try to forget what lay ahead.

As dawn began to break a sailor, spitting over the side, glanced back towards the horizon. He looked again, his eyes moving in every direction. The sea was empty. The armada was nowhere to be seen. The Mora was alone. Larger and faster than the other drakkars, she had outdistanced the rest of the fleet.

"Sire, wake up, I see none of the other vessels," garbled the sailor in a panic, tapping the Duke on the shoulder.

William's eyes opened slowly. "What, what is it?"

He smelt the sailor's bad breath and grabbing a rope, hauled himself to his feet. He leaned over the side, dipped a bucket into the sea and pulled it up to splash water on his face. The icy cold water brought him to his senses. He could see the English coast in the distance. The white cliffs at Beachy Head near Pevensey were clearly visible.

"I can see the coast. Where are we? How deep is it here?"

The sailor to whom William was addressing a volley of questions looked anxious and was not sure how to reply.

"I cannot say my Lord. But we cannot be too far from the landing point."

"Well I do not intend to land in England alone. Lower the anchor and send someone aloft. And lower the sail. We will wait."

The sailors wasted no time in carrying out William's orders. Two hauled on the ropes to lower the sail, while others threw the anchor over the side wondering whether it would reach the sea bottom. It hit the water with a loud splash and the sailors watched anxiously as the rope rapidly unwound disappearing into the deep. When the Mora shuddered to a halt they breathed a sigh of relief. They looked to the horizon. Still nothing to be seen. William did not seem too concerned. He leaned back, relaxed and began to eat. He was thoughtful, holding his medallion between his fingers. As the vessel bobbed up and down in the fast current, Odo tightened his cloak and looked at Robert.

"It is colder than I thought at sea."

"We are heading north," said Robert.

William lay back, pulled the cover over him and looked up at the clouds still moving northwards. He thought of Matilda. Would he see her again? Or the children? He began to think of their last hours together.

CHAPTER 46

After arriving at St Valery from Eu, Matilda and William had returned to his tent on the sands. It was past midday. While the last vessels were being loaded, waiting for the tide, William and Matilda walked together by the water's edge as waves lapped the shore. Matilda put her head on his shoulder.

"William." He did not respond.

Matilda nudged him. "William!"

"Eh, what is it?"

"You were lost in your thoughts."

"I was listening to the waves. It reminded me of being on the beach as a child, making patterns in the sand. The sea would rush onto the shore and when it receded there was nothing left but wet sand."

Matilda hugged William. "You are worried about this voyage to England?"

"Of course, the fear of the unknown. But it has always been my destiny to cross the sea to England."

"I always knew it to be so."

Matilda held William tightly in her arms while he continued to gaze out to sea, his mind clearly fixed on the voyage.

"What lies ahead is my greatest challenge. Either I shall be King of England or I shall be dead leaving history to judge me as a Norman adventurer who pursued a dream too far. So many good men have worked hard to prepare for this invasion and are ready to follow me across the sea into battle. I must not fail them."

"You will not fail them," Matilda assured him. "As you have not failed me. You cannot fail them, God is on your side."

William smiled at her. "So everyone keeps telling me."

Matilda kissed him. "Now come to bed. You must rest."

As they strolled back to the tent by the dunes, William stopped his manservant.

"The tide will be closing in. If I do not rise by sunset, wake me."

William and Matilda entered the tent. William unbuckled his belt and set aside his sword as Matilda helped remove his heavy clothes. He lay down on the bed and watched Matilda undress. They lay in each other's arms oblivious to the noise outside. Matilda whispered into William's ear.

"I just want to lie here in your arms. Have I told you that I knew from our first moment that we were meant for each other?"

William lay back staring up at the roof of the tent.

"You can still remember our first meeting." He smiled to himself. "I can see you now riding into the castle with your father. How you held yourself upright with your headscarf blowing in the wind. I think I fell in love at that moment."

Matilda hugged him tightly then laughed.

"And when you entered the hall to greet us and nearly tripped over I could hardly contain myself."

William frowned. "I don't recall that. I do remember you walking off though. I thought I would lose you. Oh, I have not given you my thanks for the Mora. It is a fine vessel. I know it will protect me and those who sail with me."

"You will come back?" enquired Matilda, the sudden realisation crossing her mind that this could be their last moment together.

"When the tide goes out does it not always come back." answered William reassuringly. "Now let us sleep."

It seemed much later when William opened his eyes. The noise outside had subsided. How long have I been sleeping, he thought. What time is it? He looked at Matilda still fast asleep. He gently eased her arm from his chest and slid out of bed. He pulled open the flap and saw that the day was drawing to a close. He returned to the bed, kissed Matilda on the forehead, quietly dressed and left the tent closing the flap behind him. His manservant was ready with his cloak, helmet and sword. He walked to the shore. The tide had risen. William stepped onto the Mora in the centre of the fleet, now beginning to float freely.

Matilda sat up with a start. The sound of trumpets and shouts had woken her. She looked at where William had been lying. The sheets and pillow were crumpled but the bed empty. She was alone.

"William?"

There was no reply. William had gone. She hurriedly dressed and rushed outside.

The beach had all but disappeared and what remained of the encampment, once spread out along the sands, now lay at the water's edge.

Peasants were attempting to clear planks of wood, empty boxes and rope left behind, floating in the sea. They were working cautiously to avoid being hit by debris thrown up onto the shore by the fast, incoming tide.

Matilda stopped and gazed out towards the estuary. The armada had almost reached the open sea. Kicking off her shoes, she took the hem of her dress in her hands and ran along the shore. As fast as she could, she scrambled up to the top of a dune. Dusk was falling but in the distance she could make out the vessels raising their sails. The ships' lanterns created a luminous glow, their light reflected in the water. Somewhere amongst those vessels was the Mora. Matilda just knew William was looking back and could see her.

She stood looking out to sea, her hair blowing in the wind, her face whipped by spray, as the ships became smaller and smaller. She waved and tears filled her eyes.

"Follow your dream and may God bring you safely back to me. I will be waiting for you my love."

CHAPTER 47

William was stirred from his thoughts by the shouts of a sailor clinging to the mast.

"I see them now. I can see them."

His voice woke up most of the knights who, still half asleep, began to stretch their legs and fold the blankets they had used to keep themselves warm during the voyage. Everyone's eyes were fixed on the horizon. It was a colourful sight as a multitude of colourful sails advanced swiftly towards them. The sailors waved. William got to his feet and, with his brothers, watched the approaching fleet slicing through the waves. Their sails were fully stretched as the wind pushed them ever closer to England. William looked at Odo and Robert.

"What a glorious sight. May it spread fear into the hearts of the Saxons."

William looked up at the sky and turned to the sailors.

"Raise the anchor, set sail. Now we go to England."

PART VI

CHAPTER 48

The Saxon Chronicles:
"Then came William, Duke of Normandy into Pevensey.
    This was then made known to King Harold and he then gathered a great force and came to meet him at the estuary of Appledore..."

There was a chill in the autumn air the day of 28th September 1066, with the strong southerly breeze gusting over the cliffs of the south coast of England. Since dawn, a Saxon peasant with his dog had been watching over his flock of sheep. He had chosen to take the path, which cut a wedge through the wheat fields and spiralled its way to the top of the cliffs. When he reached the summit he could feel the biting wind in his face. Far out to sea his attention was drawn to a strange dark mass, like a huge wave on the horizon. As he peered out across the water, his eyes began to widen, his mouth suddenly opened wide. His hand felt weak and he inadvertently released his staff, which clattered to the ground. He turned and, chased by his dog thinking it was all a playful game, started to race downhill towards his village frantically waving his hands in the air, scattering the flock as he went.

At 9am the first of the Norman drakkars landed on English soil and came to a shuddering, grinding halt as stones and pebbles on the beach scraped the length of its hull bringing its voyage to an abrupt conclusion. As the vessels were closing in to the shore the soldiers had their eyes trained on the cliffs, their hands on their swords ready to react if attacked. But there was no army to greet them, no welcoming party, just the sound of longships hitting solid ground. As each vessel found a space to beach, the sailors jumped ashore, and following their training, quickly made them fast. Ramps were quickly positioned to allow the provisions to be unloaded and stored on the shore.

While the first troops established defensive positions along the beach, other soldiers disembarked in an orderly fashion, allowing the knights to release their horses and lead them down the ramps, happy to be back on dry land. William was one of the first Normans to set foot in England. Wading ashore he stumbled and to avoid falling put his hands on the sand. He knelt to kiss the ground.

"By the splendour of God, this earth, which I have taken in my hands will never leave my grasp."

William stood up and let the grains of sand seep through his fingers.

"Where is the soothsayer?" William addressed the soldier nearest to him. "It is fitting that I show him my gratitude for bringing us safely through the night."

A knight carrying provisions overheard William and replied.

"Sire, he cannot be found. It is thought he must have fallen overboard."

William felt a tinge of regret but had more important things on his mind.

"Ah well. It can hardly be a loss to lose a soothsayer who could not predict his own death."

A magnificent black stallion was being guided off the Mora. Stamping his hooves on the deck in an act of defiance it leapt down onto the sand, but was kept under control by Turold. William was watching in admiration with Robert and Odo.

"Sire, your horse," said Turold, handing him the reins.

William stroked the horse and then walked it around in a circle. "Ah, my beauty. You look none the worse after a long night at sea."

Robert watched in admiration. "Such a fine gift. From one King, Alfonso of Aragon, to another King...William of England."

"With God's will. With God's will. Here, make sure you look after him."

William gave the reins back to Turold, who led the horse away.

It had taken less than two hours for the beach to become teeming with soldiers, horses equipment and weapons. But William could not allow his army to remain exposed on the shore for too long. He looked around and noticed the remains of an ancient fort.

"Someone has been here before," said a knight, following William's gaze.

William looked at him thoughtfully. "The Romans, seven hundred years ago. They called this place Anderita. They subdued the people then. We can do so now. Set up our camp within the walls where the ground is firmer."

While sentries were posted around the fortress and on the cliff top, search parties scoured the countryside to look for any sign of Saxon militia. Harold, William thought, must have left some troops to guard the coast. By evening when the soldiers had returned, they had all given William the same news. No army was to be found; neither in camps, nor in any of the villages

"Sire we have searched the coast and inland as you ordered. There is no sign of the Saxon army."

William turned to the barons, clearly relieved, hardly believing his good fortune. God had answered his prayers. "So where are they?"

CHAPTER 49

Harold was still in the North of England at Stamford Bridge. Three days after the battle, while William was establishing his base on the south coast, Harold was still celebrating with Leofwine and Gyrth, assessing the consequences of the victory over the Vikings. Although they mourned the death of their brother they agreed that Tostig's fate had been of his own choosing. He had betrayed them. It was too late to look back. The tent flap was suddenly pulled open by a messenger who seemed agitated.

"My Lord, I bring news that a Norman fleet has landed at Pevensey."

Harold looked up startled and slammed his fists on the table.

"William! Damn that Norman. How many men has he brought with him?"

"Reports say there are over four hundred and fifty vessels and an army of more than seven thousand."

"Four hundred and fifty ships and seven thousand men!" exclaimed Harold in disbelief. "Impossible. How could anyone assemble a force of that magnitude?"

"That is the information we have received, Sire," said the messenger, before bowing and leaving the tent.

Leofwine looked at his brother. "What do we do now?"

Harold's mind was racing. "What do we do? We head back south with all speed. William must not reach London unopposed."

"But the men, they are tired from battle. They need rest," argued Leofwine, concerned that Harold was expecting too much from his army.

"The fate of the nation is at stake. If we do not stop this Norman tyrant from advancing on London we shall no longer have a country. Do you understand?"

Harold reflected on what Leofwine had said.

"Give the men another two hours then get them prepared. Others will join us as we head south to London and reinforce our army."

"Would it not be wise to send word to burn the fields and starve those Normans before they have time to move inland?" suggested Gyrth.

Harold was offended by such a remark. He was King. He held the power over good or evil, between life and death.

"You ask me to devastate the land over which I have sovereignty. I cannot do that. Our own people would suffer."

Harold's plan received little enthusiasm as the order filtered through to his reluctant men that they would have to return south. The housecarls and fyrds, still exhausted from battle, had been busy collecting weapons, armour, wagons, horses and provisions left by the Vikings. Maintaining an army was no easy matter, and was expensive. Looting was not an attractive pastime, but it was normal practice for the victor to recoup whatever had been abandoned on a battlefield and could still be used.

A soldier chewing straw spat it out.

"What does he want from us? We are not superhuman."

While the housecarls and fyrds began to gather their equipment, silently cursing the King under their breath, Harold sat alone looking up at the roof of his tent, pondering his future.

CHAPTER 50

The old Roman fort made convenient quarters, but William nevertheless chose to erect a new fortress at Pevensey; one built in the style that he was used to and knew how to use. It was a typical Motte and Bailey fort and could be erected within a few days. A circular trench was dug with the earth piled up in the centre to form a mound. A wooden structure was built on top of the mound with living quarters, storage facilities and a look-out tower. A fortified palisade was then constructed around the building leaving an inner courtyard with a single gap for access protected by a timber footbridge. The trench could be filled with water to form a moat. These forts could not be compared to the stone built castles that William would ultimately build across England, but they provided a quick and efficient means to protect invading troops from attack.

The Duke of Normandy had spent forty-eight hours thinking about how to announce his presence and force Harold's hand. Once he had made up his mind he was determined to see it through regardless of the consequences. At a hurriedly convened morning meeting, William announced his intention to his commanders with a determined voice.

"Burn them out. Burn villages to the ground as a warning. But pass the word to all our soldiers that the villagers are not to be harmed. Is that clear? If I am to be their King I do not wish to make more enemies of these people than I have to."

Whatever they thought about the Duke's plan, none of the barons dared contest the decision. For the next three days Norman cavalry carried out the Duke's orders. Flames rising from several villages along the coast could be seen far out at sea. Cottages and barns were put to the torch forcing villagers to run terrified from their homes, gathering the few belongings they could carry, to seek refuge in the fields. When they had achieved their objective the knights returned to the Norman camp to report to the Duke.

Disturbed by the sound of animals outside his tent, William was somewhat annoyed at being interrupted from his discussion with Odo and Robert. Curious, he looked out to see what all the noise was about. Knights were herding sheep and pigs through the camp followed by dogs barking. When he saw the Duke, one knight stopped to explain.

"Three villages have been entirely destroyed, Sire. There were no casualties but some force had to be used." Pointing to the animals he added. "We found abundant animals and livestock. The men will not go hungry."

William waved his arm in acknowledgement and returned to his companions. It was too late to have any misgivings.

"That should send a clear signal to Harold. He will not want to see the south of England go up in Flames."

Odo had heard the knight and looked at William with an ironic smile.

"Hardly a message of goodwill to the people you hope to rule."

"That is a risk I will have to take," he replied brusquely, spreading out a map of England. They were interrupted again as William Fitzosbern entered the tent.

"Harold will soon be aware that we have landed on English soil," continued William. "If he has been forced to engage in conflict near York he will have to return south with his army of foot soldiers. This will take time and I vouch they will not relish the thought of engaging our army in another battle so soon. We have a long wait before us." William glanced behind him in the direction of the sea.

"Time to prepare for battle where we choose. I do not wish to face Harold's army with my back to the sea."

"We have found what seems to be a suitable site, just inland from the town of Hastings nearby."

William Fitzosbern looked at the map as he spoke and attempted to identify a location further east along the coast from Pevensey. William watched his friend impatiently, unable to understand precisely where he was pointing.

"You'd better take me to it."

The Duke and his loyal friend wasted no time. An hour later they were riding out of the camp at the head of a troop of knights. Their route took them through a Saxon village that had been spared. The villagers were going about their business and looked up in fear as the heavily armed Norman cavalry passed by. A knight suddenly went to a cottage in a crowded square, grabbed some straw from the roof, and held it out to William.

"Sire, I give you possession of the Kingdom of England."

They all laughed, except William.

"Shall we put this village to the torch?" enquired a knight.

"No, we have made our point," retorted William, halting his horse in front of a group of villagers. He beckoned to one of them.

"Who is your leader, an elder?"

A tall man of about sixty with long grey hair, his face weathered from working the land, dressed in torn clothes and holding a hoe stepped forward. The villagers, men, woman and children gathered anxiously behind him.

Wuldon was a Saxon. After a lifetime spent toiling the land and raising sheep in the fields and hills of the south coast close to his village, he had become accustomed to the constant menace posed by Vikings and Celts in the seemingly never ending conflict to rule England. But never had he confronted such a powerful force as these invaders from Normandy who had suddenly appeared with thousands of armed men and horses. He hesitated for a moment before plucking up the courage to face the mounted knight who had spoken. He looked William straight in the eyes.

"I am the head of this village. We beg you not to destroy our homes."

William listened to the man's plea and then, almost ignoring Wuldon, looked over him towards the villagers who had gathered around him.

"Saxons, my name is William, Duke of Normandy. I have not come as your enemy. I have come to claim the crown of England, which is rightfully mine. So long as your people do not bear arms against me you have nothing to fear and can continue to live in peace. Is that clear? Otherwise, your village will suffer the same fate as the others."

Wuldon turned to observe the villagers' reactions. They all nodded, more out of fear than respect.

"Then may God be with you."

William turned his horse and with his knights galloped out of the village, leaving the Saxons to ponder over the stark warning the intimidating foreigner had given them. They rode on until they reached a hilltop from where the sea was visible in the distance. William Fitzosbern called for them to halt. "This is it," he said pointing across the valley.

William glanced about him and took a deep breath. Then he turned to William Fitzosbern and nodded in approval.

"This Hill is where the future of England shall be decided."

William looked around the site. From the ridge of the plateau there was a wide, open stretch of land sloping sharply downhill to where a stream, hardly noticeable, meandered its way through the valley. On the other side of the stream the land rose up towards the tree covered southern hills and the coast. The valley was bordered by clumps of bushes and woodland and, on one side hidden behind undergrowth, the land fell away into a deep gully. His eyes dwelled on the landscape for a few moments before he outlined his plans to William Fitzosbern, pointing to several different sites in the valley. His mind was already visualizing the strategy to adopt for what was going to be the most vital battle he had ever undertaken. He had already calculated the distance his forces would most likely have to cover and where his bowmen would line up for their arrows to reach the enemy positions.

"We can place our archers near the foot of the slope with the infantry behind. The cavalry can bring up the rear in three divisions across the valley."

"That will give Harold the high ground," said William Fitzosbern who was astute enough a soldier to appreciate the advantage of being able to look down on the enemy.

William had considered the risk of conceding the ridge to the Saxons. Harold would be coming south from London. His route would bring him across the hill. The terrain on the far side was made up of woodland. William needed open space for his cavalry. Woodland and ditches to the left and right of the slope convinced William that his horsemen would need to be concentrated across the open field. Although they would need to climb the hill, the valley was wide. He could envisage the Saxon army of foot soldiers deployed across the ridge. As he contemplated his strategy a messenger arrived, out of breath.

"My Lord, news has reached us that Harold has defeated his brother Tostig and King Harold Hardrada in battle and they are both slain. He is already marching south to London."

William slapped his companion on the back.

"Well that removes one contender to the throne. The crown will now either be mine or Harold's. At least we know they are coming now. The English army will be on foot and cannot be fresh. But I wager they will not reach us for another week. We will move our camp here, then let the troops rest but keep them alert, ready for battle."

However confident William sounded, he could not hide a certain admiration and respect for his future adversary. Harold had led his army of several thousand Saxons more than two hundred miles and defeated the ablest and fiercest Viking Warrior and a force renowned for its fighting spirit. Even a weary and weakened Saxon army could not be underestimated.

With the news of Harold's impending arrival and his Saxon force, the two friends rejoined their troops and returned to the Norman encampment, their minds now concentrating on transporting seven thousand soldiers and two thousand horses, together with arms, material and equipment, the dozen or so miles that separated Pevensey bay from Hastings.

CHAPTER 51

After hastily erecting another fort and camp in the valley, the soldiers had time on their hands. They became bored waiting for the enemy to appear. One evening as dusk was falling two soldiers, having left the camp with a cask of beer, were lying on a hill overlooking a village. They were chewing straw as they watched a young girl gathering flowers no further than fifty metres away from where they lay hidden. She was about fourteen, very pretty, with long blond hair. Carrying the flowers in her arms, unaware she was being watched, the girl skipped down the path leading to the village. She reached a cottage and went in. The two soldiers followed her at a distance. They had been drinking and were unstable, staggering from side to side. After looking around to check that no one was watching, they kicked open the door. Inside a rather frail man and a plump woman, both middle aged and poorly dressed, were preparing to eat. They stood up and moved back in fear, cowering against a wall as the door flew open and the two men forced their way in.

"Where is she?" said one of the men, hardly able to stand.

"Who?" answered the woman, a terrified look on her face.

The other soldier hit her across the jaw with the back of his hand.

"You know who."

The woman, numb with pain, blood trickling from the corner of her mouth, moved back to block a door.

"Leave us in peace, I beg you," she pleaded in desperation.

Despite her resistance, the two soldiers dragged her screaming from the door. The man tried to intervene to protect his wife but received a blow to his head from an iron bar that one of the soldiers had concealed beneath his tunic. He collapsed to the ground, blood seeping from the wound on his forehead. The soldiers kicked open the door and slammed it shut behind them. There were screams of a child from within. The woman, supporting her bleeding husband in her arms, sat on the floor weeping.

The next morning William was in his fort discussing tactics with his brothers and several barons when the door opened and a soldier entered.

"Sire, there are some villagers here. They wish to see you."

"Villagers? What do they want?" William looked at his companions. He had more important matters to attend to than engage in conversation with Saxon peasants. "Alright, show them in."

The head villager and a group of peasants entered. William recognised the village leader. "We have met, have we not? What is the purpose of your visit?"

The Saxon elder looked nervous. He had spent a considerable part of the night awake wondering whether he should take his grievance to the Norman leader.

"Sire, we do not wish to take up your time or trouble you, but last night a child was assaulted and her parents beaten."

He lowered his head. He had thought carefully before plucking up enough courage to make such a serious accusation against the Norman invaders. "Two of your soldiers were seen leaving the village."

William's face darkened. He was visibly annoyed.

The Saxon elder stepped back worried about William's reaction.

"I will not believe that unless I see for myself."

William beckoned to a servant to fetch his horse. Together with an escort of knights he left the camp and followed the villagers in their wagon back to their village, a few miles along the coast. The wagon pulled up outside a small cottage and the leader pointed to it. William dismounted and, gesturing to his men to stay with the horses, entered the tiny cottage, lowering his head as he passed through the doorway. In the corner by the fireplace a man was seated holding his bandaged head. William placed his hand on his shoulder.

"Do you need attention? You are certain it was my soldiers who did this?"

The man shook his head and nodded at the same time.

William was then shown the rear room where a young girl was lying in bed comforted by her mother. The woman looked up, startled, as he strode in. When the child saw the stranger, his face concealed by his helmet, she screamed with fear and clutched her mother. William removed his helmet and knelt by her side. He put his hand gently on her cheek, kissed her forehead and turned to her mother.

"I too have daughters. I am sorry for this."

On his return to the camp William was in a rage. He had made his orders clear.

"I want to know who was on guard duty last night. I don't care how long it takes, but find the men who perpetrated this deed and bring them to me."

The next morning three knights were prodding two frightened soldiers with their hands bound towards the fort. Other soldiers were watching apprehensively as they passed through the camp. The knights made their presence known and made the soldiers stand and face the Duke.

"Sire, these men have admitted going to the village last night."

William looked at them.

"You defied my orders not to harm these people."

Looking down at the floor one of the soldiers plucked up courage to speak.

"We did not mean to do wrong, Sire. We had been drinking and ..."

His companion, expecting some sympathy from William interrupted. "We truly regret what happened, my Lord. You know... after a few drinks. We are sorry."

William was not in the mood for excuses.

"It is too late to be sorry. I cannot allow my authority to be ignored. And I must show these people that we are not savages.

You have brought shame on us. You came here to die in battle. You know what punishment awaits you now."

Shocked at the arbitrary sentence handed down, William's companions all stared at him but said nothing. The soldiers looked at each other, their eyes expressing fear. They sank to their knees, bowing their heads.

The next morning the Saxon villagers awoke to the sound of hammers. A gallows was being erected in the square. William was sitting on a wooden chair behind a table on a rapidly constructed makeshift platform. The two soldiers, hands bound behind their backs, were brought to the village standing in a horse-driven wagon. A soldier climbed onto the wagon and placed ropes around their necks. The villagers began to assemble in the square, chatting amongst themselves. When the square was filled with onlookers William stood and addressed the two soldiers, their heads bowed.

"You have been found guilty of carrying out a heinous crime against an innocent family and have, therefore, violated my orders. Worse, you have sinned and transgressed the laws of God. By the authority vested in me as Duke of Normandy, I sentence you to death. May God have mercy on your soul."

William nodded to the soldier holding the horses. He pulled the reins and the wagon lurched forward, leaving the soldiers dangling in space. After a few seconds the twitching ceased and the bodies, their necks twisted, hung motionless.

"Let this be a lesson. I will not tolerate any immoral behaviour or gratuitous act of violence. Saxons, if by God's will I am to be your King, let it be known that there will be no corner of this kingdom outside the rule of law."

Having made his point, William left the platform and walked towards his horse. William Fitzosbern, looking at the two soldiers hanging in the square, stood shaking his head as William walked past.

"I wonder if I will ever understand your sense of justice."

William grabbed the reins of his horse, climbed into the saddle and turned to face him. "I never asked you to understand," he replied coldly.

He eased his mount forward and with the Norman knights in pursuit, took the road to his camp while the villagers began to drift away back to their homes, leaving the soldiers' bodies swinging from the gallows. His message could not fail to have been understood.

CHAPTER 52

As dawn broke over the English countryside, with the sun low in the sky filtering through the trees, the Saxon army, snaked out along the road, was marching at a slow pace towards the coast. Despite the loss of men at Stamford Bridge and fatigue, Harold had been able to gather reinforcements on the journey south. However, his allies, Morcar from Northumberland and Edwin from Mercia, had not rallied to his cause. They had still not fully recovered from the crushing defeat inflicted on their forces by Hardrada and Tostig at Gate Fulford and were reluctant to engage in further conflict so soon.

Harold, although furious, was forced to accept their decision. Shrugging off the setback to his plans, he thought about his troops. He had been justifiably proud of his men, who had covered two hundred miles in less than ten days, between 2nd and 10th October. Back in London, he spent from the 10th to 12th October regrouping his forces and rounding up fyrds from every village along the way. His army was now some seven thousand strong - more than equal to the Norman forces.

Having followed Harold's orders to return south at all speed, the men were indeed exhausted and would need time to rest and prepare themselves for further conflict. But Harold was impatient. News of the destruction of Saxon villages along the coast had made Harold determined to prevent the Normans from advancing on London and, by the afternoon of the 13th October, they had covered the last sixty miles to Hastings hoping to catch the Norman invaders, like the Vikings, by surprise.

It was not to be. William's invasion had been the result of meticulous planning and months of preparation. He had already been in Hastings for two weeks and his forces were both rested and ready for battle. Moreover, he had already planned his strategy.

As the Saxons, marching in columns, were nearing the coast, Leofwine who had ridden on ahead, came galloping towards them. He pulled up beside his brother pointing towards the valley behind him.

"I have sighted them. They are camped just ahead over the ridge in the valley. We should bring a halt soon."

"So, they are already here and prepared for battle," said Harold, glancing around him.

"Right, set up camp here. The men are weary and can do with some rest although I fear it may not be enough. Let me take a closer look at our adversary. I would like to see their numbers."

Harold gave orders to establish camp while he and Leofwine rode off towards the ridge to take their first glimpse of the Norman army. After dismounting and leaving their horses behind a clump of bushes they crept to the top of the hill, keeping out of sight.

Below them in the valley, less than five hundred metres away, they could see the Norman camp. The reports had not been exaggerated, thought Harold, as he looked at the vast encampment, bustling with soldiers, preparing their defences. William had wasted no time, keeping his soldiers busy by cutting timber from the forests and erecting a new earth and wood fort similar to that he had left at Pevensey. To the left of the watchtower, close to a stream, Harold could make out a paddock jammed with horses. Leofwine pointed towards the camp. "They have chosen the valley. If we remain here we will be able to control the ridge."

Despite the fatigue from the long journey south, Harold felt the adrenalin rising as he looked around him and began to forge his own tactical plan in his mind. He appeared confident as he and Leofwine, keeping low, eased their bodies backwards. They mounted their horses and returned to the Saxon army, now scattered along the road sitting and eating what little food they had brought with them.

After Harold had also eaten a hasty meal with his brothers, he gathered together the Saxon commanders. Standing in the open air, they listened as he outlined his strategy.

"The Normans are here in force. It looks as if the Duke has brought his entire army. But they have chosen the valley. It will be to our advantage. We can concentrate our housecarls into defensive formations across the ridge creating a wall with shields. I have seen Norman cavalry in action. Make no mistake we will need an impenetrable defensive wall to stop them. I want the Normans to attack first, uphill. They will feel the power of Saxon battle axes. We will have to withstand their assaults and wear them down until there is an opportunity for the housecarls to charge into their ranks when they least expect it. But we need to protect ourselves against their archers. So, make sure every man knows how to handle his shield."

Harold paused waiting for the reaction to his comments. There was silence.

"By now they know we have arrived," said Harold. "Tomorrow will be a day for brave men. We will show them how Saxons fight."

CHAPTER 53

Across the valley, William was in his living quarters with his commanders going over the strategy that he believed would win the battle. Norman scouts had detected the approaching Saxon army hours before and had been following their movements as they had taken up their positions. William had anticipated that the Saxons would form a long defensive line across the ridge.

"We have been over these tactical plans repeatedly. I will go over them once more." Grouped around the wooden table in the centre of the tent, stood William's most able commanders, chosen to lead their countrymen. The Breton, Alain of Brittany, the Frenchman, Eustace of Boulogne, the Normans, William Fitzosbern, Roger de Montgomery, Walter Giffard of Longueville and the Duke's own half brothers, Odo and Robert.

When they first learnt of the Duke of Normandy's invasion plans, Alain and Eustace were not committed to his cause. However, after the Pope had given his blessing William's emissaries persuaded them that Harold could not be allowed to defy the church. The sense of adventure and potential spoils of war that would come to the victors in battle was also a determining factor in attracting men to join their armies. They had put all their efforts into the provision of ships, arms and men, and now, after the long sea voyage to England, the day of reckoning had arrived. They listened attentively to the Duke as he explained his strategy.

"You, Alain will take the Bretons and the men from Maine and Poitiers on the left while Eustace, will ride with the French and Flemish on the right. My brothers will lead the Normans in the centre, by my side."

Eustace had seen the Saxons preparing their defences.

"If the Saxons hold the ridge their strong shield wall will be hard to break down."

"It is the task of our archers and infantry to inflict sufficient damage to enable our cavalry to breach their defences," continued William persuasively.

"Most Saxons have never seen Norman cavalry in action. Mobility is our strength, so use it." He paused and looked at his commanders. "Does anyone have any questions?"

Roger de Montgomery answered for everyone.

"I think we all know what is expected of us."

The Barons all nodded their agreement.

"One more thing," said William. "Do not underestimate the Saxons or their King. When Harold was with me in Normandy he proved his courage. If the Saxons could endure a forced march and still defeat an army of determined Viking warriors, they know how to fight."

Odo glanced towards William.

"At least the weather is holding and the ground should be firm for our cavalry."

William grinned. "God is on our side, didn't you know?"

Alain of Brittany appeared anxious. He had been persuaded to join the invasion as a means of securing closer ties with Normandy. But was now having misgivings about leading his forces into unknown territory.

"I just hope we can limit our losses. Saxon axes can be devastating."

"I fear that there will be many casualties on both sides," said William softly, stating what everyone knew in their hearts.

They were distracted by voices and the sound of boots outside. After announcing their presence three soldiers entered pushing before them two Saxon prisoners. One of the soldiers addressed William.

"We caught these two men spying, my Lord."

They were prodded towards William who walked around them, looking them up and down, studying their clothing and arms. They were young, no more than eighteen, small and scruffy, their clothes muddy and torn from crawling through bushes.

"So, this is how you intend to do battle." He looked around at the barons.

"They don't look too fearsome do they?"

William ran a hand over their tunics and took a sword out of its scabbard, pointing it towards their throats. The two men were visibly scared. They knew what Viking justice was but had no idea what the intimidating Norman was going to do with them.

"Well, you have seen our camp and discovered your enemy. Now what shall we do with you?"

William remained silent, watching them for a few minutes, leaving the Saxons time to contemplate their fate.

"I think I am going to let you return to your camp unharmed. But I want you to take a message."

The Saxons appeared relieved as William called for a scribe. On his arrival William sat down and slowly dictated a message. When it was complete, the scribe handed the scroll to William who placed his seal on it, rolled it up and handed it to one of the Saxons.

"Go tell your King that I am prepared to divide the Kingdom. If he accepts my offer there will be no need to spill either Saxon or Norman blood. I must have a reply before the sun rises. Do you understand? Before sunrise. Now go."

The spies nodded, needing no encouragement to leave the tent. Norman soldiers accompanied them to a point halfway up the hill where they were within one hundred and fifty metres of the Saxon positions. There, the Normans bid farewell to the Saxons, leaving them to continue on foot, while they returned to the camp in the valley. William watched the two Saxons until they had reached the ridge and disappeared from view, then addressed his Barons.

"We have a long night ahead of us. Let me rest. But wake me if there is news from Harold."

The Barons took their leave. Alone in his spartan quarters, William, unbuckled his scabbard and lay his sword on the camp bed. Holding the medallion in one hand he knelt down and, placing his other hand over his heart, looked upwards.

"Oh Lord, I place my faith in you to avoid bloody conflict between Saxons and Normans. But should no sign reach us by morning, then, show us that good can conquer evil. We are all mortal and ask for your protection in our just cause to see us safely through the battle which confronts us."

Orrin Smith Sc

CHAPTER 54

The Saxon Chronicles:
"... and William came against him unawares before his people were assembled. But the king nevertheless strenuously, fought against him with those men who would follow him; and there was a great slaughter made on either hand."

The 13th October 1066 drew to a close. Scattered across the English hillside, fourteen thousand men were passing their last night before battle; men from different villages, distant regions, even different countries. They comprised all manner of medieval society: Saxon earls, Norman, Breton and Flemish barons, knights, squires, archers, mercenaries, professional warriors, fyrds and peasants, even men of the church; good men all gathered together to battle for what they believed was a rightful and just cause.

The torches in the camps were clearly visible to both sides. In the valley, the Norman camp was subdued; smoke rose from the makeshift kitchens as cooks prepared the evening meal and soldiers waited in line to eat; others were celebrating mass, checking their weapons and trying to sleep. Geoffrey, Bishop of Coutances, a colleague of Odo, passed around the camp listening to confessions and giving benediction to those who sought comfort. Turold continued to play the fool attempting to bring some light relief to the men. But he too was not in the mood and finally wandered off to tend to the horses. On the way to the stables he picked up a stick and, pretending it was a sword, began to slash at imaginary enemies. Discarding it as he reached the horses, he lay down on some hay and was soon asleep.

In stark contrast, the Saxon camp was noisy and boisterous as soldiers spent the night drowning their fears in an orgy of drinking and singing. The muffled sound could be heard down in the valley. One soldier, well and truly inebriated, was looking at the locket worn by a young housecarl seated next to him.

"What's that round yer neck?"

Erwulf looked down and took the locket in his hands, proud to be wearing it.

"It's for good luck. My girl made it for me. When this is over I'm going to return to my village and we will marry."

"Bah! Marriage," blurted the first soldier, wiping his hand across his mouth. "It ties yer down."

Gradually, the torches fizzled out and knights, soldiers, fyrds and peasants on both sides lay down to sleep or dream of home. A strange silence fell across the hillside and down into the valley.

The year 1066 moved on to the 14th October. The weather was warm for the autumn season. As the hazy sun rose above the trees, casting its warmth across the hillside, the Saxon and invading troops were gradually waking, quietly dressing and adjusting their coats of mail. After taking a rapidly prepared meal and hot drink they put on their helmets, selected their weapons and on the orders of their commanders, began to move into their allotted positions.

King Harold of England and William Duke of Normandy had planned their strategy according to their own time-honoured tactics and experience. Only one of them would be proven right.

Seven thousand Saxons were massed shoulder to shoulder across the ridge in a formidable defensive wall formed by the interlocking of Saxon round shields, up to ten men deep and more than two hundred metres wide. Their conical shaped helmets glinted in the sun, the reflection sending flashes of sunlight towards the Normans. The Saxon front lines, which would have to bear the brunt of Norman attacks, were comprised of the trained housecarls, armed with battleaxes and swords. Behind them Harold had assembled a force of fyrds, with an array of weapons ranging from scythes and knives to rocks and slings. Harold had placed himself at the highest point behind the defensive wall, next to the Saxon standard. His brothers Gyrth and Leofwine had taken up positions on each flank. From his high viewpoint, Harold could see his Norman rival in the valley as he rode to the front of his army in full battle dress on his black Spanish stallion.

Sensing that the battle was about to begin Harold prepared to address his soldiers. He glanced up at the sky to see two falcons circling overhead. His eyes followed their flight as they swept downwards, before disappearing from view into the trees. Standing on the trunk of a felled tree next to his standard bearer, who was flying the flag with a dragon depicted on it, he raised his sword and, speaking with a forceful voice, made what would be his last declaration.

"Brave men of England. The fate of a nation depends on each and everyone one of us doing his duty this day. No foreign invader can tell us how we should live, or how we should die. Your valour will be rewarded by victory, whatever the sacrifice. I, your King, fight by your side with honour."

The pounding of Saxon shields and cheers could be heard by the Norman army, who were spread across the valley at the foot of the hill.

The Norman front line comprised more than three thousand foot soldiers split into three columns in perfect formation, armed with swords and carrying shields. Behind them, kneeling, were archers with longbows and crossbows, more than one thousand strong, their quivers, with a full complement of arrows, placed beside them. At the rear the cavalry, with over two thousand horsemen, was lined up in three divisions across the valley.

Harold could see that William had divided his forces in three formations; the Breton and Poitevin cavalry under Alain was on the left flank, the French and Flemish led by Eustace on the right flank, and in the centre the Normans, led by their Duke and his brothers.

Like the Saxons, the Norman forces wore knee length chain mail over their leather jerkins and their heads were also protected by the battle-tested, metal conical helmets with a protective wedge covering the nose. However, the Normans' secret weapon was its cavalry. Each horseman was armed with a lance, designed for use when charging, and a sword for close combat. The horses had saddles shaped with high pommels to provide stability when they were wielding swords and lances in battle. Each contingent flew its banner and the knights could be identified by the coat of arms on their almond shaped shields. The Saxons had never faced cavalry, let alone two thousand highly trained and disciplined Norman knights. In the centre of the Norman position, their royal standard had been raised, flapping in the wind; a red flag with the figures of two gold lions representing the House of Normandy.

After making certain that his army was ready, William joined his brothers, Robert and Odo, at his central command post. By Odo's side was Geoffrey of Coutances. As a noble Norman, loyal to the Duke, he had been asked by fellow bishop, Odo, to participate in the invasion and now found himself in the middle of an English field waiting for the Duke to signal the start of a conflict which he had no doubt would be bloody and brutal. He thought back to the cathedral he had helped to build in Coutances and his appointment as Bishop in 1048. It all seemed so long ago and far away. As a man of the church, Geoffrey was carrying the papal banner in his hand.

"There has been no sign from the Saxon camp?" asked William.

"Nothing at all," replied Odo.

William looked downcast.

"We gave Harold a choice. He has chosen to ignore our offer of peace. May God forgive him."

On the ridge, Harold continued to watch William's movements. He could see him clearly as he rode to the front of his army and turned to face his men. William stood up in his saddle but the Saxons were too far away to hear what he was saying.

"Brave men until this day is over time will stand still. Nothing that has gone before has been so daunting. Nothing that comes after will be so decisive. Outright victory is our only recourse. Retreat is impossible and defeat means death and the end of a noble cause. Never have we needed so much courage."

William placed his hand over his heart. "God is with you. Your strength will come not from the height of castle walls or depth of a moat, but from within your heart."

Odo eased his horse towards William. In his hand he held a mace, not a sword, because although members of the clergy could take part in conflict, religious laws forbid them from penetrating flesh and causing blood wounds.

"We pledge our trust in God that he will watch over us and grant us victory in the name of the Pope."

Having taken the papal banner from Geoffrey of Coutances, Odo raised it skywards before attaching it to his saddle. This left his hands free. He took the mace in one hand and his shield in the other.

William reached down to his neck and grasped his medallion. He raised it to his lips and kissed it. Then tucking it back inside his chain mail, he gripped his sword and slowly raised it above his head.

9.00am: Before he had time to lower it, a lone horseman suddenly rode out from the line of cavalry to the front of the Norman forces facing the Saxons. As William watched in astonishment, he raised his sword and pointed it in the direction of the Saxon wall. Gently kicking his horse with his heels he began to trot slowly towards the Saxon line. As the rider slowly made his way uphill, thousands of Saxon eyes peered out from behind their shields wondering what he expected to achieve. He increased his speed to a gallop and time seemed to stand still until he was almost on top of the shield wall. That was as far as he got.

The Saxons roared in unison as they let fly a hail of stones, axes, knives and lances. There was a clash of metal and tearing flesh as both horse and rider collided with the shields and were brought down. While the horse struggled to its feet and galloped off, seemingly unscathed, the man lay motionless, red streaks seeping through his chain mail. Silence returned to the hillside.

William turned to Odo. "Do you know that man's name? He has sacrificed his life for our cause."

Odo, not able to fully comprehend what had happened just shook his head.

William looked at his army and raised his sword again. Rising in his saddle, he brought his sword downwards. "GOD HELP US." His voice echoed across the valley.

9.20am: With a deafening cry, the battle began. On William's signal the Norman archers, kneeling in line, unleashed a volley of arrows over the heads of the foot soldiers towards the Saxon line. As the swishing noise grew louder and the sky darkened under a cloud of arrows, a shout went up on the ridge.

"Shields up, shields up." In one co-ordinated movement the housecarls instinctively ducked and raised their arms, holding their shields above their heads, feeling the power of the arrows thudding into them or flying over their heads. The wall did not budge. William then ordered the Bretons to charge uphill from the left. But the Saxons were prepared. As they approached the ridge the Bretons were met with a torrent of stones, swords and axes that crashed onto them. With mounting casualties they had little choice but to retreat downhill leaving dead and wounded comrades on the field where they had fallen. The screams of those slashed, decapitated or struck by Saxon weapons rang in their ears as they raced back to their lines.

After ordering another volley from his archers that had little more effect than the first salvo, William once again ordered the Bretons to attack. He turned to his cavalry. On his signal, Eustace of Boulogne eased his mount and with the right wing contingent in three rows behind him, slowly advanced uphill. Simultaneously, William Fitzosbern began to lead the Norman cavalry in the centre.

As the Saxons on the left faced another attack from the Bretons, further along the ridge their comrades could feel the earth begin to tremble beneath the hooves of French and Norman horses. As the trotting turned into a gallop the muffled sound increased and, with a wave of Norman horses surging towards them, beads of sweat began to pour down the faces of some of the younger and inexperienced Saxons, who were peering over their shields.

Erwulf, in the second rank of housecarls, was thinking about the lifeless body of the Norman lying just below him on the hillside, the sound of horse and rider crashing down before him still echoing in his mind. His leg muscles were taught and ached from the march south but he was proud to have served King Harold and been with his comrades these last weeks. They had not let down their King. He thought about the Vikings. He had killed some, perhaps three or four. It had come at a cost. He could still feel the pain from the gashes on his arm and leg where Viking swords had caught him. They had not had time to fully heal. Now he would kill some of the Norman invaders and push them back into the sea. What a story he would be able to tell Ayla when he returned to his village to marry her and raise a family.

The beads of sweat dripped onto his collar and his tongue felt dry as the noise became louder and louder until the sound of hooves was rendered inaudible by the thunderous clash of swords, shields, lances and axes as the Norman cavalry met the

Saxon defensive wall. An array of weapons and stones flew out from behind the shields, bringing down both riders and horses. The damage inflicted by the Saxons spared neither men nor horses, but the French and Norman lances were also finding their targets. At one point part of the shield wall began to weaken, but as soon as one soldier fell, another took his place. The line was holding. Harold watched the first attacks from his position behind the Saxon defensive line. A soldier called out to him.

"We have repelled their first attacks, sire, the line is holding well."

Further along the line as the attack ended, the beads of sweat continued to drip down onto Erwulf's collar.

"Hah, looks like we beat them off," he mumbled to the soldier standing next to him, trying to put on a show of bravado.

"They were just testing us," he replied, the fear apparent in his voice.

Erwulf's thin smile rapidly faded.

10.20am: Retreating downhill, the remnants of a troop of cavalry that had been decimated after failing to make any impact on the shield wall, had ridden too far east and inadvertently found themselves heading into a gully, concealed by bushes. The ground was marshy and the horses began to slip and slide bringing down their riders. Housecarls on the ridge spotted their opponent's predicament as they attempted to extract themselves from the quagmire. Despite Harold's orders to hold the line some felt it was too good an opportunity to miss and raced downhill into the gully, leaping upon the helpless Normans. Using swords, spears and axes they caused havoc amongst the stranded knights, before clambering out of the deadly ditch and returning safely to their own lines, leaving the dead and the wounded where they fell, unable to crawl out. By the time William had sent in reinforcements it was too late. The gully had turned into a graveyard. It had been aptly named: Malefosse – 'the devil's pit'. It was to be William's only reverse that day.

11.00am: East of the ridge, unable to make any impact on the Saxon defences and with their losses increasing, the Breton foot soldiers began to withdraw downhill. Suddenly a rumour began to circulate that William had been killed. One Breton soldier, losing his nerve, shouted out. "The Duke is dead. All is lost." This led to other Bretons starting to panic and take flight, fleeing in all directions.

Without waiting for orders, a troop of housecarls wielding battle axes left their line in pursuit causing disarray amongst the foot soldiers. As more Normans and Bretons withdrew in haste passing the message that William had died, a figure on a horse suddenly appeared galloping across the valley. The knight removed his helmet and raising his sword bellowed out to his men.

"Who is spreading such blasphemous lies? Am I not immortal? Get back into the fight or I will cut you down myself."

Seeing their Duke on his horse and in their midst the soldiers stopped and cheered, chanting William's name as they raised their swords. William, charging in all directions, was shouting orders reorganising his men and grouping them into a solid formation at the foot of the hill. Having raced out of their protected lines to chase the Bretons, the contingent of Saxon housecarls had by now distanced themselves from the ridge and were exposed. William, quickly assessing the situation, ordered his foot soldiers to block their retreat and charge into their ranks. The Saxons found themselves quickly isolated and surrounded, unable to call for support. In the hand to hand fighting that ensued, a spear pierced the neck of William's horse and it fell to the ground bringing down its rider. William pulled himself clear and saw his horse dying. He stroked its head. The black stallion was lying quite motionless, its eyes expressing pain and fear.

"We will not see the end of this day together. What fate to make such a long journey from Spain, only to die on this English hill…"

Before finishing his sentence, William had to move quickly to fend off some Saxon soldiers, who may have recognised him and thought they could bring the battle to a premature conclusion. He was forced to fight on foot until Robert suddenly arrived holding out the reins to another horse.

"Mount, you cannot defeat the Saxons on foot."

Robert rode off, leaving William to climb into the saddle of his new horse. He took a final look at his dead stallion before being forced to fend off more housecarls. Like many of the Normans he had expected that the Saxons would show little mercy to their enemies, but the savage treatment to their revered horses had come as an unpleasant surprise.

Despite closing ranks the Saxons found themselves outnumbered. One by one they fell beneath Breton and Norman swords until the whole group was annihilated. From his position on the ridge Harold had watched in dismay as his elite housecarls were being decimated. There was little he could do without weakening his defences. His whole strategy had been based on wearing down the Norman attacks. The shield wall had to hold.

11.30am: The battle had been raging for over two hours and the sun was now high in the sky. There was a lull in the fighting. William now had a clear idea of Harold's tactics. The Saxon wall had held up well against his attacks. The mobility of the Normans was hampered by the Saxon defence. It was only when the line broke and the Saxons were forced to fight in the open that William could use the cavalry as he had planned. From his position on the ridge, Harold also understood the Norman tactics.

"Exactly as I envisaged," he shouted to his brothers. "Don't weaken our line. Hold our position."

In the valley William, his face and armour by now splattered with blood, had rejoined Robert and ordered him to locate Odo and his commanders. William had dismounted and was standing on the trunk of a fallen tree gazing towards the Saxon lines when they arrived. The Normans had made no progress and were suffering substantial losses. While they were assessing the situation and discussing tactics, a knight rode up to William.

"Sire, there is a rider approaching from the ridge."

12.00pm: They looked up and saw a lone rider trotting towards their lines. He had his arms held high to show he was an emissary not a belligerent.

"Let him pass," shouted William to his archers. The rider passed through a gap in the Norman lines, rode up to William and his barons, and dismounted, diligently making sure that the Normans could see he was unarmed. Two knights closed in as he approached William.

"I bring a message from King Harold for Duke William."

William stepped forward. "Speak." The knight looked at the Norman standing before him. "So this is the Duke of Normandy," he thought to himself not over impressed by his appearance.

"Explain the purpose of your visit."

"The King says that by now you must realise how futile it is to pursue this combat. Your army will be destroyed. You will be spared from further unnecessary losses if you all turn around and return to your ships and Normandy."

"I see," said William, looking around at his brothers. "Tell your King he has seen nothing yet. He has usurped the crown of England, violated his oath to me and opposed the Pope. Renounce the throne and I promise that he will be treated with respect."

"Is that your answer?"

"It is my only answer."

"Let me return with him to talk with Harold," implored Odo.

"No, I can't afford to risk you taken hostage. Send a couple of soldiers with my answer. And ask him, in the name of humanity, to allow all those still on the field, and not yet departed from this world, to receive treatment."

Harold had been watching attentively from the moment he had sent his messenger down into the valley. He saw two riders leave the Norman lines and ride uphill. As they approached the Saxon line he beckoned to his men to let them through, hoping the Duke had seen the logic of his proposal.

12.50pm: The response was not what either Harold or William had hoped for. William had no intention of returning to Normandy empty handed and Harold would not stand down. Both men knew that the hostilities would rage until one of them capitulated or fell on the field of battle. However Harold had agreed for bearers to be allowed to tend to the wounded and remove corpses and weapons from the hillside. This gave time for both armies to take a short rest, conserve their energy and reflect on their next move. It was clear to both Harold and William that more blood would be shed that afternoon.

William's brilliance and experience as a military commander would now be tested. He had perceived how the housecarls had been drawn out of the wall when the Bretons retreated. From behind the Norman line he barked out new orders to his brother, Robert, and in turn to Alain of Brittany, Eustace of Bouogne and William Fitzosbern. He remembered his strategy at Varaville against King Henry of France.

"We will advance on two fronts towards the Saxon defences. Then the Bretons and French will turn around and feign retreat. Hopefully this will draw more Saxons from their lines. Once they are isolated I will attack with my cavalry."

William bid his commanders to rejoin their troops. As he watched them ride off across the valley he muttered to himself.

"Harold will regret defying me again. Only one of us will walk away from this field."

Chapter 55

The Saxon Chronicles:
"There was slain King Harold and Leofwine the Earl"

1.45pm: William ordered Robert to join Alain with the Bretons, William Fitzosbern to link up with Eustace and the French, while he and Odo would remain with the Normans in the centre. After another hail of arrows thudded fruitlessly into the Saxon shield wall, the Flemish and French contingent led another charge. As soon as they were met with the anticipated Saxon response of axes, spears and stones, they turned and fled. Suddenly with a shout, a troop of housecarls surged out of trees on the left of the ridge and charged downhill in full cry after the retreating French. Harold looked furious.

"Who ordered them to attack?"

Wielding swords and axes, the housecarls raced into the valley in pursuit of the Normans. By the time they had reached the lowest point in the valley, the Normans were already climbing the slope on the other side. As soon as they saw the Saxons still chasing after them, the Normans halted and turned to face the oncoming soldiers. William, at the head of his Norman cavalry, had been watching from a distance. Making sure that the whole Saxon line had not left their lines in pursuit, he waited until the charging Saxons had run out of steam and seemed disorganised. Then he gave the signal to charge from behind trees into the right flank of the housecarls. The Saxons suddenly found themselves not only facing foot soldiers with swords coming from the higher ground but horsemen coming at them from their flank. Cut off from their army and surrounded, the Saxons desperately fought to survive, exchanging blows with axes, swords and lances.

Suddenly, William noticed a tiny figure on a horse charge into the fray and with his sword raised cut down two Saxons. But a huge warrior, on foot, dragged him off the horse and plunged his sword into his squirming body as he lay on the ground.

"No. No!" William's scream of anguish could almost be heard above the din of battle. He galloped towards the body, jumped off his horse and picked up the small, motionless figure. Placing him across his saddle William rode back to the Norman camp with all speed. With the help of servants, he lowered the body onto a makeshift table.

"Turold," he said the pain evident in his tone. "What were you doing?"

"I have always been a clown, listening to people laughing at me." Turold spoke softly and with difficulty as blood seeped from his lips. "I wanted to do something, be somebody. Will you tell Goles I fought by your side."

"I promise," said William with a lump in his throat.

"And tell him...tell him, I'm sorry." Turold's head dropped. William nodded, and placed his hands over Turold's eyes to close them. As he rose to his feet he looked up at the sky and said a prayer, then slowly walked back to his horse to return to the battle.

Attacking the remnants of the Saxon housecarls, William's horse was once again brought down and he found himself on foot for the second time that day. He was forced to engage in hand to hand fighting using his shield as a weapon. Turold's death had provoked a profound anger and William found a hidden strength to repel the Saxon attacks.

Gradually, the training of the Norman troops began to tell and they overpowered the exhausted housecarls, who were suffering substantial casualties. The remnants of the Saxon force had no choice but to try and reach the safety of their position on the ridge, making a disorderly retreat as best they could, struggling up the hill and leaving bodies either dead or wounded scattered across the field.

2.45pm: Both sides needed to review their tactics and count their casualties. Harold had watched in dismay as the elite of his army, the housecarls, had broken out of their defensive line, been cut down and forced to retreat. William too had been frustrated by the Saxon defensive shield wall.

William Fitzosbern found William mounting his third horse of the day. They all looked exhausted and dirty.

"We still cannot breach the Saxon line. They are managing to hold the ridge."

William then barked his most significant order of the day, one that would determine the outcome of the battle.

"Tell the archers to aim higher and find targets behind their defences. The arrows are merely bouncing off Saxon shields."

"If we don't breach the wall soon we will run out of arrows," said William Fitzosbern.

William had also realized that with no bowmen amongst the Saxon forces they could not retrieve any enemy arrows so he had provided his bowmen with extra compliments of full quivers. William Fitzosbern passed along the line ordering the archers to advance closer to the ridge and raise their bows higher. The line moved forward. There was little risk of being attacked with the Saxons massed behind their defences. Hundreds of bows were now pointing towards the clear sky. At the order to fire, a solid cloud of arrows flew high into the air. The faint swishing sound grew louder and louder and as the Saxons looked up, a barrage of shafts rained down behind the defensive wall right into the heart of Saxon defences. Raising their shields to protect themselves, the Saxons were now exposed to the Norman archers wielding deadly crossbows. Kneeling in front of the bowmen, they waited for the right moment, took aim and fired straight into the wall of bodies. Chain mail armour offered little protec-

tion to anyone struck by a well-aimed crossbow bolt. The luckless victims were literally flung backwards by their force.
Caught between crossbow fire and arrows raining down from
the sky, the Saxon defensive wall began to weaken. Harold had
not anticipated that Norman arrows would reach his own position. Taken by surprise as the arrows were falling behind the
Saxon defences, he received a direct hit from an arrow, which
pierced his eye. He collapsed to the ground in agony. With his
head protected by his conical helmet it was a lucky strike for the
Norman archer who had fired it. Whoever he was, he could
never have imagined that when his fingers released the thin shaft
from his bow to fly high in the sky towards the Saxon line it was
about to change the course of history.

A knight, seeing the King's predicament, rushed to his assis-
tance. On seeing the wound he called out in desperation.
   "The King is hit! The King is hit!"
   Harold was holding the arrow, his face grimacing with pain
as blood, oozing from the wound, ran through his fingers.
   "Find Leofwine and Gyrth. Bring them to me," he stam-
mered, his voice faltering.
   "They have been slain, Sire," said the knight dejectedly.
Harold tried to rise and grasp the knight by the shoulders.
"Both my brothers dead? Then all is lost. What irony."
   Harold's mind reeled back to that calamitous day in Bayeux
two years earlier when he had given his oath to William.
   "That England's destiny should be fixed by a single Norman
arrow. My oath to William? Did I sin? Where is my sword? If I
am to die, let me die like a King. Help me up."
   Two knights struggled to help Harold to his feet but he cried
out and fell back his sword across his body.
   "The King is mortally wounded. I fear our cause is lost."
   "What purpose then in prolonging this battle?"
   "It is for each one of us to make his own decision."
   Looking down at their King the two knights knew that they
had very little time left to make up their minds.

4.30pm: It did not take long for word to pass among the house-carls and fyrds still holding the ridge that their King had been seriously wounded. The Saxon wall became demoralised as a wave of Norman, Breton and Flemish troops charged uphill on foot or on horseback. Courageously, the housecarls and fyrds tried to repel every attempt to dislodge them from their positions but finally the shield wall buckled and then caved in as the Normans managed to break through and split the defences, slashing and killing as they went. Saxons started to flee in disarray, chased by Norman cavalry.

A small contingent of Norman knights breached the Saxon command post on the ridge. They found Harold's prostrate body still clinging on to life and taking their own personal revenge, plunged their swords into his chest. Then, they grabbed the Saxon banner, ripped it to pieces and thrust the Norman standard into the ground, raising their arms in triumph and cheering as it fluttered in the wind over the bloody hillside.

CHAPTER 56

The Saxon Chronicles:
"...and the Frenchmen had possession of the place of carnage, all as God granted them for the people's sins."

6.00pm: The battlefield was now quiet. Bodies lay everywhere, some silent and motionless, some moaning in pain. Soldiers moved around the site separating those clinging to life from those departed, removing corpses, carrying the wounded and gathering weapons. Nobody seemed bothered about the looting as boots, weapons, rings, belts, clothing, and anything that could be recovered, were stripped from the dead. Robert found William, bloodied, sitting against a tree next to his horse.

"You are hurt?"

William looked up at his brother.

"No, bloodied, but the Seigneur has saved me from serious wounds."

William Fitzosbern appeared, followed by Odo and Geoffrey of Coutances.

"I thank God you have been spared," said William, relieved that his kinsmen and friends had survived the carnage.

"Harold has been killed, as have his brothers, Leofwine and Gyrth." announced William Fitzosbern. "The Saxon army is fleeing and we can march on London without further resistance. Nobody can contest your right to become King of England now."

William held out his hand to Robert and with his help found the strength to stand up. Tired and bloodstained he looked around at the carnage. Although evening had brought a cool breeze, the day had been warm and the stench from decaying corpses was already permeating across the valley. Followed by his companions he slowly walked around the battlefield looking at the bodies strewn everywhere; men and horses lying lifeless on the hillside, or barely alive, with amputated limbs, beyond hope, their injuries from axes too serious to save them. Those suffering relatively minor flesh wounds caused by blades, arrows or lances were more fortunate, waiting in the hope that someone would tend to their wounds. Odo and Geoffrey, dressed in their black robes, stopped from time to time in order to give the dying the last rights. William stepped over a Saxon soldier. The grass had turned a shade of red beneath his body and there was a gaping hole in his side. He was still clutching his sword. There was nothing to distinguish him from the hundreds of other corpses except for a locket with a sheep's head carved from wood hanging around his neck. William stooped to take it in his hands, then laid it carefully back upon his chest.

"I have seen enough blood for one lifetime," said William to his companions. "Now it is over I still cannot fully appreciate the enormity of what we have accomplished."

William reached the ridge. Some of his foot soldiers were grouped around the Saxon position where the Norman standard had been planted into the ground. They were staring down at the body of a Saxon warrior. He was lying on his back, his arms by his side, his legs straight. The soldiers parted when they saw William and let him through.

Geoffrey of Coutances was standing over the body.

"Harold?" he enquired as he moved closer. Geoffrey turned and nodded. William approached the body. King Harold's chest had turned red with gaping holes where Norman broadswords had pierced his chain mail. His face was still concealed by his helmet. William knelt down beside him, took the helmet in his hands and slowly removed it allowing Harold's long hair to fall below his shoulders. His face was distorted and bloody with a hole where his right eye had been. William placed his hand on his forehead. Before rising he noticed the arrow, broken in two, lying by the body. He picked up the broken shafts and half smiled, remembering the gifts he had exchanged with King Edward many years before.

"If only you had sent word we could have avoided this bloodshed," he sighed, raising his eyes to the sky. "If there is one single task I have now it is to reconcile Saxon and Norman citizens and unite this nation."

William turned to a Norman Knight standing next to him. His name was William Malet, Lord of Graville. William put his hand on his shoulder and uttered what was perhaps his most humane order since the landing in England.

"I knew this man. If he sinned it was for his country. Give him a decent burial."

As William walked away, William Malet glanced towards the group of soldiers standing around watching and pointed his finger at two of them.

"You. Help me lift his body. It will be our task to give this man a Christian burial."

Nobody paid attention to the two falcons, which had been circling overhead and had flown down to land on Harold's chest.

Daylight was fading before the Norman, Flemish, Breton and French barons rejoined William. They had been occupied with the laborious task of counting casualties and prisoners, comforting the wounded and tending to the troops. The flames from burning torches, held aloft by soldiers, could still be seen creating strange patterns across the hillside. Although exhausted, William wanted to express his tribute to the barons who had put their trust in him. When they had gathered together he walked among them acknowledging their contribution.

"You have shown immense courage. Together we have emerged victorious and I owe all of you a debt of gratitude, which shall be honoured. But we must not forget this day."

Odo stepped forward and put his hand on William's shoulder.

"With God's will we have prevailed. History will remember this day and your victory. Here the people will not know you as the Duke of Normandy but William the Conqueror, King of England."

William smiled at his brother's compliment. But he was modest enough to realise that while the battle may have been won, he was not yet a King and, even if the people had been conquered by force, he would now need to earn their respect to rule.

"You speak of God's will, Odo. Then we shall build and dedicate an abbey on this site to thank the Lord for bringing us safely through this battle. It will serve as a lasting memorial to all these good men, Norman, French, Breton, Flemish - and Saxon, who have perished on this field. And so that future generations can remember what took place here this 14th day of October in the year of our Lord 1066."

CHAPTER 57

The following morning at daybreak, despite the cold and threatening grey sky, William was riding his horse alone along the shore. He looked out to sea thinking of his homeland and Matilda. They seemed so far away. When would he see her and his children again? And there was another no less important factor he had to come to terms with. Even wearing the crown of England, William would still be the Duke of Normandy and with all the power his status granted, he remained the vassal of the King of France.

Despite Odo's optimism William had no illusions as to the task ahead. He knew there was much to be done before his mission was over. London still stood between him and the crown. With sixty miles of unknown territory to cross and a potentially, hostile population to deal with, he could ill afford to waste more time on the coast. The army had to be mobilised once again to march on towards the final goal.

Pockets of blue appeared between gaps in the clouds as they drifted across the sky. William dismounted at the water's edge, bent down and cupping his hands collected a mound of sand. He smiled as he let the tiny grains seep between his fingers. He reached down and pulling his sword from its scabbard stuck it deep into the sand. Then he knelt and, holding the hilt with both hands, looked up at the sky.

"Lord, with your will and protection I have ruled Normandy for thirty-one years; three decades of plotting, scheming and bloodshed. Against all the odds you have given me the strength to overcome my enemies and conquer England with the blessing of the Pope. I pray that you can grant me the wisdom to bring together the people of this Kingdom, forgive the manner of my birth and let me be a good Christian and just ruler." He thought for a moment. "Is this the end or just the beginning?"

The advice given to him as a child by the Abbot at Jumieges flashed through his mind.

"Learn to be just and magnanimous with your people and your enemies."

William stood by the water's edge observing the waves as they washed over his boots before receding. Reaching down, he picked up a pebble and threw it far out to sea. He watched the ripples form as it skipped over the surface before sinking beneath the water.

CHAPTER 58

In the crypt of Bayeux cathedral Odo and the novice were devoting their attention to the final section of the tapestry.

"So what happened after the battle?"

Odo took a deep breath. His mind went back to the events of the last two months of the year 1066 and the coronation in the new Abbey at Westminster presided over by Aldred, Archbishop of York.

"We marched on London and then...and then...oh what a magnificent day that was. To see my brother crowned on Christmas day. William I, King of England."

Odo frowned and altered his tone. "All of us who followed him were granted titles and estates. But after he took the crown, my brother became a changed man."

"But how did the tapestry come to be here?" asked the novice.

Odo, eliminating the thoughts of his brother and imprisonment from his mind, proudly answered the novice's question.

"Memories fade with the passage of time. But this was one moment in history never to be forgotten. It had to be preserved for eternity. While I was in England I had it commissioned and executed by weavers in Canterbury. When I returned I brought it with me to adorn the walls of this cathedral. It has been here ever since."

Odo paused and looked at the novice.

"What are you called?"

"Friar Aubert, Seigneur."

"Help me put the tapestry back into the vault. Be careful."

But there is still some of the tapestry left to see," exclaimed Aubert.

"Another time," responded Odo curtly, leaving the novice slightly perplexed at his sudden haste to return the tapestry to the vault. He could not help wondering what the final section contained, but decided not to insist.

They delicately folded the tapestry, placed it back in the chest and closed the lid. At the request of Odo, Aubert turned the key and locked it.

"Aubert, are you are going to be ordained in this cathedral?"

"Yes, I hope so."

"I must leave again, on a long journey to Jerusalem. I want you to give me your word that whatever happens to me you will not let the tapestry leave the cathedral."

"You have my word, Seigneur."

Odo placed his hands on Aubert's shoulders.

"Then I entrust the keys to you."

Aubert clutched the keys. Together they lifted the chest, now secured, and slid it back into the vault. Aubert pulled the vault door and slammed it shut with a loud clang, the sound reverberating around the crypt. He then turned the key in the lock, once again sealing the tapestry in the blackness and silence of the crypt.

The end. Or is it the beginning?

Epilogue

William the Conqueror, who became King William I, ruled England for twenty-one years until his death in 1087. His reign ended the domination of the Saxons, Celts and Vikings. As the most powerful man in England, he brought stability and unity to the country, exercising justice through the rule of law. Throughout his twenty-one year reign he continued to exercise his power over the Duchy of Normandy, no mean feat considering the warring factions he had to deal with on both sides of the English Channel. His marriage to Matilda was a faithful union, lasting until her death on 1st November 1083. She had not yet reached fifty. She bore him ten children and the dynasty so formed led to a succession of Kings of England. The Norman and French influence and culture that exerted itself across the country changed Anglo Saxon society forever and endured for almost three centuries.

To act as a deterrent and protect the Normans from aggression or rebellion by the Saxon population, who greatly outnumbered his army, William ordered the construction of castles throughout the Kingdom. These fortresses were built of stone from Caen and followed the Norman tradition of square keeps with massive stone walls. In the capital, London, he built the White Tower, still standing inside the walls of the Tower of London on the banks of the river Thames. Being a pious man, he also built monasteries throughout the land, appointing Norman monks and abbots to encourage worship amongst the people. Many of these churches still exist today, a testament to the quality of medieval stonemasons. William's abbey at Battle was demolished during the reign of Henry VIII, but later buildings such as the Gatehouse, remain. A memorial in the village, near the town of Hastings, marks the site where Harold was killed. Lanfranc was rewarded for his loyalty. In 1070, after

Stigand had finally been removed, William appointed him Archbishop of Canterbury.

As the last conqueror of England, William of Normandy changed the course of English history. The coat of arms of the House of Normandy depicted two gold lions against a red background. One hundred years later King Richard I - the Lionheart - added a third lion. Representing Normandy, England and Aquitaine, they still appear on the Royal Standard of England, which flies over the country's Royal Palaces.

He left a legacy that has been handed down to the present day. Men were sent out to every corner of the kingdom to survey the estates and possessions of all landowners including their livestock, to be documented as a means of identifying the wealth of the country. It was called the Domesday Book. Today, it can be found in the National Archives, at Kew in London.

Bishop Odo never did see the Tapestry again. He died in Sicily on his way to the Holy Land to join the first Crusade. His body lies in the Cathedral in Palermo. As for the tapestry, it lay hidden for over four hundred years before it next saw the light of day. It was removed from the cathedral but was protected by successive generations. Under Napoleon, it was housed in the Paris Louvre. It is believed it was then taken back to Normandy, but during the Second World War it was once again transported to Paris, to be hidden in the vaults of the Louvre, until it returned to Normandy permanently.

Arguably the most important surviving document commemorating the Norman Conquest of England, legend has it that following the battle of Hastings, William's half brother, Bishop Odo of Bayeux, commissioned the tapestry in Canterbury to record the events of this historic period. Known in France as Matilda's tapestry, it is considered unlikely that William's wife, as both Queen of England and Duchess of Normandy, would have been able to undertake such a monumental oeuvre, given her royal commitments. The last section of the Tapestry is missing. It has been suggested that it had been ripped off during the French revolution, but the mystery has never been resolved.

Today the Tapestry is in the French city of Bayeux, housed in its museum as part of a permanent exhibition dedicated to the Norman Conquest of England. After nearly a thousand years, the jury is still out on the final judgement of the Norman Conquest and the consequences of William's twenty-one year reign as the last invader of England. The term 'conquest' would be a more appropriate definition of the profound cultural transformation he imposed on the kingdom and the people, rather than the outcome of the battle of Hastings.

William, Duke of Normandy, was crowned King of England on Christmas Day 1066, fitting for someone who had spent a considerable part of his adult life overseeing ecclesiastical reform in his native Normandy, rebuilding the abbeys, monasteries, churches and cathedrals devastated by the Vikings. He would pursue his quest in England and the vestiges of Norman castles, churches, and cathedrals can still be found across the country, a lasting tribute to the religious convictions of this man, who finally came to terms with his illegitimate origin.

The military experience he gained over more than twenty years in his native Normandy, and the victory at Hastings, showed up the shortcomings in the then basic and static Saxon fighting tactics. He brought to England a brand of modern warfare based on mobile cavalry under the command of knights and the use of archers. This had a lasting impact on the art of war.

History shows him to have been cruel and vengeful to his enemies and righteous and generous to his friends. He had a reputation of being avaricious, which the Saxons learnt at their cost. Yet, whatever his shortcomings, as a monarch he laid the foundations of a society based on the feudal system, bringing with it agrarian and religious reform, common law, land tenure, architecture and culture, legacies which have been handed down to this day. William and Matilda are still together in Caen. His tomb is in the Abbey of St Etienne while she was laid to rest in the Church of La Trinite.

It is ironic that Earl Godwin, whose dream was to extend Saxon domination and who opposed so vehemently King Edward's Norman friends, was actually instrumental in the transformation of English society to the French language and culture. When he endorsed the claim to the throne of Edward the Confessor and arranged for his daughter Edith to become Queen, he could not have envisaged that Edward's Norman upbringing would eventually lead to more than two hundred and fifty years of French and European influence and culture. Since 1066 no other aggressor has ever invaded England.

ENGLAND AND NORMANDY IN THE 11TH CENTURY

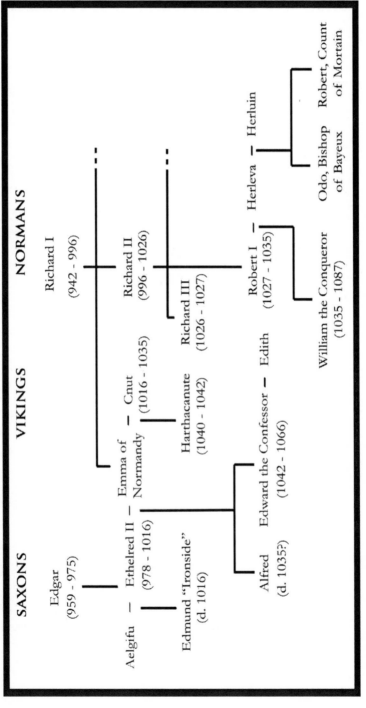

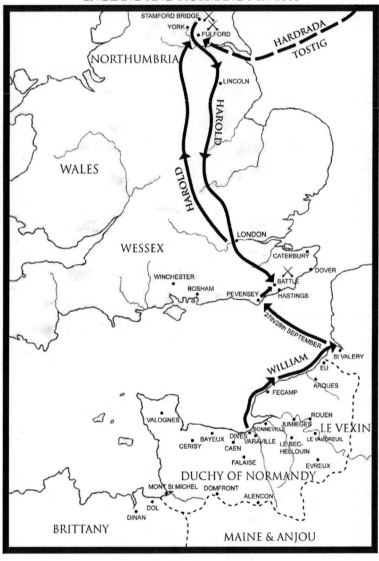

ENGLAND AND NORMANDY IN 1066

STAMFORD BRIDGE
YORK
FULFORD
HARDRADA
TOSTIG
NORTHUMBRIA
LINCOLN
HAROLD
WALES
HAROLD
LONDON
WESSEX
CATERBURY
DOVER
WINCHESTER
BATTLE
BOSHAM
PEVENSEY
HASTINGS
27th/28th SEPTEMBER
St VALERY
EU
ARQUES
WILLIAM
FECAMP
ROUEN
VALOGNES
JUMIEGES
LE VEXIN
BONNEVILLE
BAYEUX DIVES
LE VAUDREUIL
CERISY
VARAVILLE
CAEN
LE BEC-
HELLOUIN
FALAISE
EVREUX
DUCHY OF NORMANDY
MONT St MICHEL
DOMFRONT
ALENCON
DOL
DINAN
BRITTANY
MAINE & ANJOU

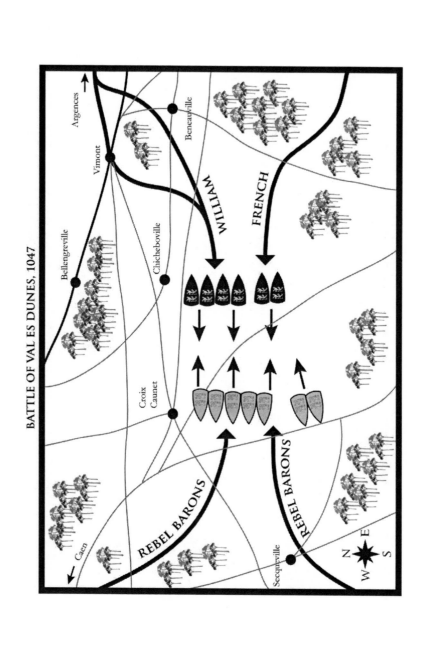

BATTLE OF VAL ES DUNES, 1047

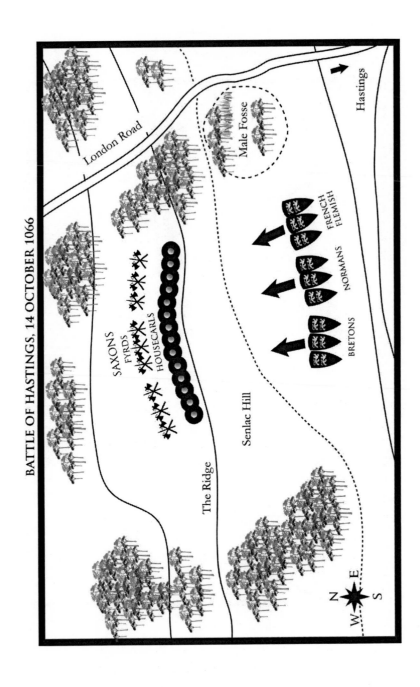

BATTLE OF HASTINGS, 14 OCTOBER 1066

Appendix:

Principal characters

Normandy
Adele of Flanders: Matilda's mother and sister of Henry 1 of France
Alun of Brittany: William's ally
Anselmo Baggio: future Pope Alexander 11
Baldwin V Count of Flanders: Matilda's father
Conan of Brittany: William's enemy
Eustace of Boulogne: William's ally
Fulbert: William's grandfather
Geoffrey of Coutances
Geoffrey Martel: Earl of Anjou died 1060
Goles: Dwarf and court jester
Heleva: (Arlette) William's mother
Henry: King of France died 1060
Herluin of Conteville: Arlette's legal husband and father to Odo and Robert
Lanfranc: Bishop of St Stephens and future Archbishop of Canterbury
Matilda of Flanders: William's wife
La Mora: William's personal longship
Norman archers: Vital division of Norman war machine
Norman cavalry: Renowned horsemen and fighters
Norman Longships: Following tradition of Viking drakkars
Odo: Bishop of Bayeux and William's half brother
Osbern: Guardian to the young William
Pope Leon 1X
Robert the Magnificent: William's father
Robert: Comte de Mortain and William's half brother
Robert Champart of Jumieges: Confident of Edward the Confessor and Archbishop of Canterbury

St Rasilphe and St Raven: The sacred saints
Turold: Dwarf and Court jester
Walter and Osbert: Arlette's brothers and William's uncle
William: Duke of Normandy and King of England 1027-1087

Loyal Barons:
Hubert Count of Ryes
Roger de Beaumont
Roger de Montgomery
Walter Giffard
William Fitzosbern Fitzarfast

Rebel Barons – the Richardists:
Grimoult de Plessis
Guy de Bourgogne
Hamon de Creuilly
Neel de Saint Sauveur
Ranulf de Briquessard
Raoul Taisson
William Talvas Lord of Belleme

England
Aldred: Bishop of York
Edith: The Queen, daughter of Godwin and sister to Harold
Edith Swanneck: Harold's "wife"
Edward the Confessor: King, died 1066
Edwin: Earl of Mercia, grandson of Siward
Fyrds: Peasants conscripted to fight when called upon
Godwin: Father in law of King Edward, Harold and Tostig's
	father, died 1053
Gyrth: Harold's brother died 1066
Hakin and Wulfnoth: Harold's kinsmen held hostage in
	Normandy
Harold Godwinson: Son of Godwin and King Edward's
	brother in law. The last Saxon King, died 1066
Harold Hardrada: The last great Viking King, died 1066

Housecarls: Elite Saxon soldiers
Leofric: Earl of Mercia
Leofwine, Harold's brother, died 1066
Morcar: Earl of Northumbria, grandson of Leofric
Siward: Earl of Northumbria
Stigand: Priest and Archbishop of Canterbury
Tostig: Harold's brother, died 1066
The Witan: Body of Saxon notables, custodians of the law

Principal sites:

Normandy and France:
Alencon: Fortress on Anjou border
Anjou: Region to the south of Normandy
Arques: Castle in Northern Normandy
Bayeux: Town in Normandy, home to Bayeux Tapestry
Bec Hellouin: Abbey where Lanfranc studied
Bessin and Cotentin: Regions in Normandy
Bonneville: Castle near Dives where William resided during
    preparations to invade Britain
Breteuil: William Fitzosbern's domaine
Brionne: Domain of Guy de Bourgogne
Caen: Town on banks of the Orne river where William built a
    citadel
Cerisy: Norman abbey built by William's father
Cluny: Monastery in central France
Dinan: Fortified town in Brittany
Dives: Small port where William built his armada
Dol: Fortress in Brittany
Domfront: Fortress on Anjou border
Eu: Castle on Normandy's north border, where William was
    married
Falaise: Castle and birthplace of William
Grestain: Burial place of Arlette, William's mother
Jumieges Abbey: Monastery where King Edward and Robert
    where brought up

Le Vaudreuil: Norman castle where William's father often resided

Mont st Michel: Abbey on Border with Brittany

Mortain: Castle of Robert, William's half brother

Mortemer: Site of battle in 1054

Poissy: Town on Seine where French had court

Ryes: Domaine of Hubert, William's ally

Rouen: Town where William established court

St Valery: Estuary from where William sailed to England

La Trinite and St Etienne: Two abbeys built in Caen as promised to the Pope in exchange for agreeing to marriage

Troarn: Small Abbey used by William prior to invasion

Valognes: Region of Cotentin where William was nearly assassinated

Val es Dunes: Site of major battle in 1047

Varaville: Site of major battle in 1057

Vexin: Region of France, bordering Normandy

England:

Anderita: Roman name given to Pevensey

Battle: Site of Battle of Hastings 1066 and construction of Abbey

Bosham Abbey: The church where Harold prayed prior to his journey to Normandy.

Derwent: River in Yorkshire

Dover: Important castle protecting coast

Fulford: Site of battle near York in 1066

Ouse: River near York

Pevensey: Landing place of William's armada

Stamford Bridge: Site near York where Harold defeated Hardrada and Tostig in 1066

York: Most important Anglo Saxon and Viking city in Northumbria

Westminster Abbey: Abbey built by Edward the Confessor that is also his burial place.

Winchester Palace: The Royal Court

Peter Fieldman was born in London, England in 1943. After a career in international real estate he took up journalism, but has only recently begun writing novels and screenplays. Married to an Italian, and with two grown up sons, he spends his time between Paris, Florence, Madrid and Aix en Provence.

The contents and characters in this book have been extracted from actual historical events and the Saxon chronicles. Otherwise, the historical facts have been adapted or modified for the purposes of artistic interpretation.

Back cover design: Norman Coat of Arms
William's vessel the Mora from the Bayeux Tapestry

Lightning Source UK Ltd.
Milton Keynes UK
28 August 2010

159140UK00001B/48/P